P9-DHL-260

Contents

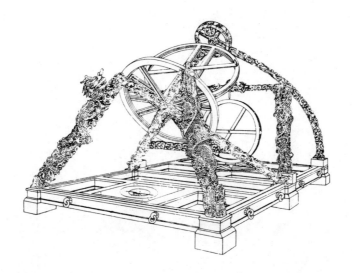

THE CHINESE ASTROLOGY WORKBOOK

THE
CHINESE ASTROLOGY
WORKBOOK

How to Calculate and Interpret Chinese Horoscopes

by

DEREK WALTERS

THE AQUARIAN PRESS

First published 1988

© DEREK WALTERS 1988

British Library Cataloguing in Publication Data

Walters, Derek, *1936–*
The Chinese astrology workbook.
1. Chinese astrology
I. Title
133.5′0951

ISBN 0-85030-641-8

*The Aquarian Press is part of the Thorsons Publishing Group,
Wellingborough, Northamptonshire, NN8 2RQ, England*

Printed in Great Britain by Woolnough Bookbinding Limited,
Irthlingborough, Northamptonshire

3 5 7 9 10 8 6 4 2

Introduction

The Chinese Astrology Workbook is intended to be a practical guide to the calculation and interpretation of astrological horoscopes according to the methods used by the ancient Chinese.

The expression 'Chinese Astrology' is often used to mean any kind of fortune-telling used by the Chinese. Even when the term is limited to those methods which draw up horoscopes based on the date of birth, this still includes several different branches of fortune-telling which would scarcely be recognized as astrology by Westerners. But the word 'astrology' means knowledge of the stars, including the 'wandering' stars – the planets – and this is the understanding of the word accepted in this workbook.

The Chinese are certainly very familiar with horoscopes cast according to the time and date of birth, though the methods used to draw up such horoscopes usually have little or nothing to do with the stars or planets themselves. Today, most of the so-called 'astrologers' in China either practise conventional Western astrology, or one of the fortune-telling methods peculiar to the Chinese, such as Ming Shu, which is based on the calendar and therefore indirectly related to the movements of the Sun and Moon, or perhaps even a form of horoscope computing based on the *I Ching*.

Yet despite its present comparative rarity, in ancient times true astrology was a highly organized science in China, the office of Grand Astrologer being one of the highest positions at the Emperor's court. Unfortunately, as a science, planetary astrology became debased through the centuries, one of the reasons being the continuing influence of the Western methods brought to China by Buddhist scholars.*

There was another reason, too, for the demise of genuine Chinese astrology. It is now well known that the Chinese of about two thousand years ago kept accurate and highly detailed records of astronomical events such as eclipses, the motions of the planets and comets, and that these have been an important source of historic information for present-day astronomers. Most important astronomical discoveries, whether in China or in the West, have been the result of centuries of meticulous observation of the heavens. Because

---

*Readers who are interested in the history of the subject will find more information in the Aquarian astrology handbook – *Chinese Astrology*, also by Derek Walters.

of the extreme antiquity of Chinese astrology, it has happened that with the passage of great lengths of time, some of the basic astronomical principles laid down by ancient astronomers appeared to be false. Actually, they were inaccurate, but only in so far as the inaccuracies could only be observed after centuries had passed. What might have been true once was no longer the case after a few thousand years had elapsed. The astrologers, both those of the court and the monasteries, still kept to their old tables, and what was once an exact science based on observation became a purely academic theoretical exercise which no longer had any relevance to the actual motions of the heavens.

By the early twentieth century, authentic Chinese astrology had been all but completely submerged into the Western system, and apart from the dressing up of Western terms (such as the names of the signs of the zodiac) in Chinese guise, there was rarely any difference in the appearance of a horoscope whether it was cast in Nanjing or New York.

For these reasons, this workbook presents a method of astrological calculation and interpretation which is based on the original source material for Chinese astrology, but modified for present-day use. In order to achieve this aim, the processes used by the ancient astrologers have been carefully examined in the context of the astronomical data which were current during the lifetimes of the sages. Examples of methods for calculating planetary positions have been modified as if the astronomers, armed with their textbooks, and no other knowledge, had been transported two or three thousand years forward in time.

But bringing an ancient astrological system into line with the requirements of the present age involves the creation of new and intriguing factors.

Ancient Chinese astrology was principally a matter of observation on the spot, and so there was never any necessity to make allowances or adjustments to the time and place of birth. But an expanded world means that the subject of the horoscope can no longer be deemed to be from one particular spot on the earth's surface – that is, the Emperor's Palace at Cheng Tu – but might be from anywhere on the planet. Just as important, however, is the necessity to take into account the fact that people live in the southern hemisphere, something which was not known to the ancient Chinese. Fortunately, the grammar of ancient Chinese astrology provides for this contingency, even to the extent of having a name for the missing region – the Jade Green Palace.

There is also, of course, the important matter of the date to be used. Chinese horoscopes traditionally carry a version of the Chinese date expressed in an eight-character formula called the Four Pillars, the four pillars in question being the hour, day, month and year of birth. In a horoscope based on purely astronomical data, the Four Pillars have only a partial significance, and as the complications of calculating the Chinese date are so onerous, an argument could be put forward for dispensing with this additional task. Nevertheless, the method for finding the Four Pillars is given not only for the sake of completeness and authenticity, but because there are several important aspects of Chinese divination which relate to them. One of these is Ming Shu, a form of numerological astrology, and familiar through the names of the animals of the 'Chinese Zodiac' (Rat, Ox, Tiger, and so on, which are neither constellations nor stars). More importantly for the 'stellar' astrologer concerned with the stars and planets, is the method called by the Chinese the Purple Crepe Myrtle Divination, that is to say, Great Bear Astrology, which is described in some detail in the earlier part of this book.

The reader who wishes to be concerned solely with planetary astrology, however, could, in theory, omit the sections on the calendar and Great Bear Divination, and move straight to the chapters on planetary astrology, relating the positions of the planets directly to the Western calendar. But this would mean leaving behind much of the essence of Chinese astrological reasoning, and the understanding of the subject would be much the poorer. For this reason, following the section on the Stems and Branches of the calendar, familiarity with the system will be assumed throughout.

Finally, of course, there is the matter of the relevance of the horoscope for the present day. The omens and auspices decreed by the ancient sages have been interpreted for contemporary use. It is not the Western custom to offer sacrifices to ancestors – other than occasional grave-tending, but donations are frequently made to charitable causes. We may not need to fear the wrath of the Emperor, although it may be prudent to be circumspect in our dealings with those in positions of authority. Marauding hordes may not invade our frontiers – but burglars can threaten the sanctuary of our homes.

Life and death, joy and sadness, wealth and poverty – these are always with us, whatever the century, and whatever the culture. And these are principally the matters which have always been the concern of Chinese astrology.

1.

Practicalities

The basic data needed to compute any astrological horoscope are the time and place of birth.

There are many astrological philosophies, and their reasonings are as varied as the methods used to compute the horoscopes themselves. Some believe that it is the actual stellar bodies which influence our lives, in the way that the actual physical presence of the Moon affects the tides. The ancients averred that the stars and planets were the abodes of the gods who direct our destinies. Modern thinkers, taking a more scientific approach, assert that the cycles of the planetary motions are merely coincidental indicators of the rhythms of existence.

But in essence, all philosophies agree on one basic principle: two people may be born at different times in the same location; two people may be born in different locations at the same time; but no two people can be born at the same moment in the same spot.

From this principle stem the two criteria: (1) the time of birth, and (2) the place of birth. Astronomically speaking, since the heavenly bodies are in constant motion, at any moment of time the locations and the positions of the stars and planets in the heavens are unique, irrespective of location. Since the Earth is a sphere, any two points on its surface must be orientated in different directions, irrespective of time. Thus, at the time of birth, the angle of direction is unique, and at the place of birth, the time is unique. The Chinese express this by saying that mankind (Jen) is midway between Heaven and Earth.

In order to draw up a horoscope, it is therefore necessary first to express the moment of birth in a convenient form, and secondly to establish the place of birth in a manner which relates to the time.

The first of these principles (time), since it establishes the positions of the heavenly bodies, is regarded by the Chinese as the Heavenly Principle, and shown in the horoscope by the Heaven Plate. The second principle (location) being determined by the birth-place on Earth, is called the Earthly Principle, and expressed in the horoscope by the Earth Plate. In ancient times, the shape of the Heaven Plate was circular, and the Earth Plate square. However, Chinese horoscopes of the Yuan Dynasty and later (equivalent to our late Middle Ages) adopted a compromise shape that was neither circle nor square, and used instead a distinctive twelve-sided figure which when divided into sections is reminiscent of a spider's web.

In preparing the horoscope, there are three basic processes:

1. Establishing the time and place of birth;
2. Drawing up a chart;
3. Interpreting the horoscope.

The Western astrologer has no difficulty with the first of these processes, but when preparing a Chinese horoscope, it has to be remembered that the Chinese calendar is not regular. Furthermore, it will not come as a surprise to discover that there are basic techniques and terms to be learnt which have no direct equivalent in the West. For this reason, before embarking on the actual process of drawing up and interpreting a horoscope, the practical section of this workbook deals with the Chinese calendar and then continues, in Chapter 2, with what might seem a puzzling irrelevance – the system of Stems and Branches.

The Calendar

Because the Chinese calendar is directly related to astronomical events, it plays a central role in Chinese astrology – so much so that it is vitally important to be absolutely familiar with the calendar's essential principles.

The main reason why the Chinese calendar is so much more complex than the Western one is because the phases of the Moon do not match the length of the year measured by the Sun, and the Chinese calendar takes this into account. As if that wasn't complicated enough, the Chinese also have several other ways of reckoning the days and seasons, and all these calendars run simultaneously. This might seem alarming, but this very complex topic is introduced to the reader step by step.

For the moment, here is a brief outline of some of the components of the Chinese calendar to be found in the annual Chinese almanac. It may appear daunting at first glance, but it is only necessary to skim through the following paragraphs at this stage, in order to become familiar with the various terms used. Each topic is dealt with in closer detail in the appropriate section.

A Chinese horoscope should give most, if not all, of the following data pertaining to the moment of birth:

1.   The Western date
This is expressed in numbers, as for example, the second day of the third moon (i.e. the second of March). Names are not given to the months.

2.   The Lunar date
This is also expressed in numbers, exactly in the same way as the Western date, with which it could be easily confused. So, for example, the second day of the third moon might mean the second day of the third month of the Chinese lunar calendar (which

might be, say, 15 April) or else 2 March. Again, there are no names in regular use for the Chinese lunar months, and the reader is advised to use the code letters, given in a later section, as a means of differentiating the two calendars.

Of course, either of these systems may be used for establishing the moment of birth. It might seem that the Chinese calendar would be unnecessary for the casting of a horoscope chart, but as the reader will discover, there are aspects of Chinese astrology which relate directly to such things as the phases of the Moon, which can be found directly from the Chinese date.

There are also other factors which are of fundamental importance in many aspects of Chinese astrology, in particular the Stems and Branches. (These are explained fully in a later section, but a note about them is given below.)

3. *The Western days of the week*
Western days of the week are noted by Jih, the Sun, for Sunday, and the numbers 1 to 6 for the days Monday to Saturday.

4. *The Ten Stems*
The Ten Stems are ten numbers which follow each other in sequence, like the names of the days of the week, and have been used to number the Chinese days since the beginnings of recorded history.

5. *The Twelve Branches*
The Twelve Branches are a second series of numbers running parallel to the ten stems, forming a complete cycle of sixty stem and branch combinations. In the earliest calendars, six of these sixty cycles constituted a year (360 days).

6. *The Twenty-Eight Hsiu*
Each day is also named after one of the twenty-eight 'lunar mansions' or Hsiu, remarkably unequal divisions of the ecliptic (the apparent belt of the sky through which pass the Sun, Moon and planets) into twenty-eight sections. The Hsiu names when applied to the daily reckonings only occasionally coincide with the actual astronomical positions of the Moon. As there are seven days in a Western week, it follows that the Hsiu fall into four groups of seven, which coincide with the days of the Western week. This is explained at length later.

7. *The Twenty-Four Solar Terms*
An important factor of many astrological calculations, the twenty-four solar terms are divisions of the solar year, based on the solstices and equinoxes. Two such solar terms form a division roughly equivalent to one sign of the Western zodiac.

8. *The Twelve Indicators*
A further series, which does *not* run in regular order, is the Chien Chu sequence of Lucky and Unlucky days. They are twelve in number, one of which, according to complex rules, is repeated, thus forming a sequence of thirteen. As $13 \times 28 = 364$, it is believed that they were meant to be combined with the twenty-eight Hsiu to form a regular calendar.

9.   The Magic Square Number

The days, months and years are counted off by nines in reverse order, which forms the basis of Nine House Divination. In the widest sense of the term, it is a form of astrology since the day count is based on rotation of the Earth, the month count on the phases of the Moon, and the year count on the orbit of the Earth. This topic, however, is outside the scope of this book.*

Review

It will probably be helpful to remind the reader of the points covered so far.

1.   The calendar has a central function in Chinese astrology.
2.   Chinese months do not have names.
3.   Chinese months are related to the phases of the Moon.
4.   The days are counted according to each of the following systems:
     - (a)   The day of the lunar month.
     - (b)   The Stem (one of ten regular signs).
     - (c)   The Branch (one of twelve regular signs).
     - (d)   The Hsiu (one of twenty-eight regular signs).
     - (e)   The Twelve indicators (one of twelve irregular signs).
     - (f)   The Magic Square Number (one of nine numbers).
5.   The year is divided into:
     - (a)   Months, according to the Moon;
     - (b)   Twenty-four Terms, according to the Sun.

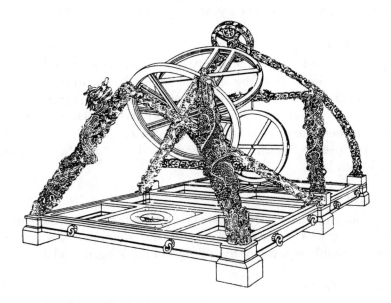

---

*Those readers who are interested in this side-road of Chinese astrology, will find it described in *Chinese Astrology*, pp. 47–9, and pp. 255–60.

2.

The Stems and Branches

It is impossible to discuss Chinese astrology, or any other aspect of Chinese science, without reference to the 'stems and branches'. The stems are a series of ten characters, the branches a similar series of twelve characters, which are used in the way we might use algebraic letters or roman numerals respectively. But they have a much wider application, as well as having a significant and specific astrological function. As every year, month, day and Chinese double-hour has its own stem-and-branch combination, the student is urged to become familiar with these two sequences at the earliest opportunity, and to regard them as the ABC of Chinese astrology.

The Ten Heavenly Stems are:

Chia	Yi	Ping	Ting	Mou	Chi	Ken	Hsin	Jen	Kuei*
1	2	3	4	5	6	7	8	9	10

[*Pronounced: Ja, ee, bing, ding, moe, jee, geng, shin, rzhen, gway]

The Twelve Earthly Branches are:

Tzu	Chou	Yin	Mao	Ch'en	Ssu	Wu	Wei	Shen	Yu	Hsü	Hai**
I	II	III	IV	V	VI	VII	VIII	IX	X	XI	XII

[**Pronounced: Tz, joe, yin, mao, chen, soo, wu, way, shen, yu, sheu, hie]

Throughout this book the convention is adopted of referring to the stems by the figures 1–10, and to the branches by the roman numerals I–XII. Thus stem 5 is Mou, branch V is Ch'en.

The stems and branches are usually combined together, to produce a series of sixty double-signs. This is actually much simpler than it sounds.

The two sequences commence together, thus: Chia-Tzu (1-I), Yi-Chou (2-II), Ping-Yin (3-III) . . . until Kuei-Yu (10-X) is reached. The stem sequence then begins again, while the branch sequence continues up to Hai (XII), thus: Kuei-Yu (10-X), Chia-Hsü (1-XI),

Yi-Hai (2-XII). Then the branch sequence begins again while the stem sequence continues, thus: Ping-Tzu (3-I), Ting-Chou (4-II), and so on, until both sequences end together with Kuei-Hai (10-XII).

It will be noticed that an even stem must always appear with an even branch, an odd stem with an odd branch. The Chinese refer to odd and even as *yang* and *yin*, thus certain pairings, i.e. those which combine yang stems with yin branches and vice versa, are never found. This makes it possible to devise a couple of simple exercises which help to familiarize the stem-and-branch terms.

Preliminary Exercise (Answers below*)

1. Which of the following pairs of signs are not possible?
   (a) 2-II, (b) 3-VII, (c) 4-IX, (d) 5-X, (e) 6-I, (f) 7-XI
2. Which of the following stem-and-branch pairs is not possible?
   Chia-Yin, Ping-Mao, Mou-Wu, Keng-Tzu, Jen-Shen, Hsin-Yu

The Sexagenary Sequence

It is sometimes convenient to refer to the stem-and-branch pairs by their position order in the sequence of sixty possible combinations. Thus Chia-Tzu (1-I) and Yi-Chou (2-II) are numbers 1 and 2 respectively in the sexagenary sequence; Jen-Hsü (9-XI) and Kuei-Hai (10-XII) are 59 and 60. Tables A and B show all the sixty possible combinations.

Table A: To find the sexagenary Number from the Stem and Branch

Branch:			Stem: 1 Chia 甲	2 Yi 乙	3 Ping 丙	4 Ting 丁	5 Wu 戊	6 Chi 己	7 Keng 庚	8 Hsin 辛	9 Jen 壬	10 Kuei 癸
子	I	Tzu	1	—	13	—	25	—	37	—	49	
丑	II	Ch'ou	—	2	—	14	—	26	—	38	—	50
寅	III	Yin	51	—	3	—	15	—	27	—	39	—
卯	IV	Mao	—	52	—	4	—	16	—	28	—	40
辰	V	Ch'en	41	—	53	—	5	—	17	—	29	—
巳	VI	Ssu	—	42	—	54	—	6	—	18	—	30
午	VII	Wu	31	—	43	—	55	—	7	—	19	—
未	VIII	Wei	—	32	—	44	—	56	—	8	—	20
申	IX	Shen	21	—	33	—	45	—	57	—	9	—
酉	X	Yu	—	22	—	34	—	46	—	58	—	10
戌	XI	Shu	11	—	23	—	35	—	47	—	59	—
亥	XII	Hai	—	12	—	24	—	26	—	48	—	60

*Answers to preliminary exercises: 1 – (c), (d) and (e); 2 – Ping-Mao.

Table B: To find the Stem and Branch from the sexagenary Number

1	1–I	16	6–IV	31	1–VII	46	6–X
2	2–II	17	7–V	32	2–VIII	47	7–XI
3	3–III	18	8–VI	33	3–IX	48	8–XII
4	4–IV	19	9–VII	34	4–X	49	9–I
5	5–V	20	10–VIII	35	5–XI	50	10–II
6	6–VI	21	1–IX	36	6–XII	51	1–III
7	7–VII	22	2–X	37	7–I	52	2–IV
8	8–VIII	23	3–XI	38	8–II	53	3–V
9	9–IX	24	4–XII	39	9–III	54	4–VI
10	10–X	25	5–I	40	10–IV	55	5–VII
11	1–XI	26	6–II	41	1–V	56	6–VIII
12	2–XII	27	7–III	42	2–VI	57	7–IX
13	3–I	28	8–IV	43	3–VII	58	8–X
14	4–II	29	9–V	44	4–VIII	59	9–XI
15	5–III	30	10–VI	45	5–IX	60	10–XII

Familiarize yourself with the stem-and-branch combinations by working these examples.

What is the sexagenary number for the following stem-and-branch pairs?

(a)   3-I, 4-VI, 5-XI, 6-II, 7-V.
(b)   Chia-Shen, Yi-Hai, Ping-Ch'en, Jen-Tzu, Kuei-Wei.

What are the stem-and-branch combinations which have the following sexagenary numbers?

1, 5, 14, 36, 60.

What are the Chinese names for the stem-and-branch combinations which have the following sexagenary numbers?

11, 22, 25, 44, 58.

Popular Names for the Stem-and-Branch Combinations

Although the stem-and-branch terms described above have been current in Chinese astrology for many thousands of years, more popular names have become attached to the stems and branches. In Mongolia particularly, official documents and Imperial Decrees bore these popular names for the dates in preference to the more literary style of stems-and-branches.

The Ten Heavenly Stems take the names of the Five Planetary Elements, thus:

Stem	Element		Stem	Element
1, 2	Wood		7, 8	Metal
3, 4	Fire		9, 10	Water
5, 6	Earth			

Usually, the fact that there are only five elements to be allocated to the ten stems does not matter, simply because the branches can only be paired with the stems which they match in polarity. However, if it is ever necessary to specify a particular stem by its element, this is done by adding the yin-yang quality. Thus, yang-wood is stem 1, yin-wood stem 2, yang-fire stem 3, and so on.

The Twelve Earthly Branches take the names of twelve animals, thus:

Branch	Name
I	Rat
II	Ox
III	Tiger
IV	Rabbit
V	Dragon
VI	Snake
VII	Horse
VIII	Sheep
IX	Monkey
X	Cock
XI	Dog
XII	Pig

Notes

1. The sequence of animals will be found easy to memorize if the animal names are grouped in threes: rat–ox–tiger, rabbit–dragon–snake, horse–sheep–monkey, cock–dog–pig.

2. Sometimes you will encounter references to the Cat as an alternative to the Rabbit; this is not correct and it is never known as such by the Chinese.

The element-animal names are primarily used to reckon the years, and any sexagenary number can be expressed as an element-animal combination. So the sequence begins wood-rat, wood-ox, fire-tiger, fire-rabbit, earth-dragon, earth-snake, and so on, following the same double sequence as the stems and branches, except that the elements are repeated in pairs throughout.

Converting the Date

The first task which a Chinese astrologer has to perform, when constructing a horoscope, is to convert the Chinese date into the Four Pillars. For Westerners, unfortunately, the process is made more complicated by the initial necessity to convert the Western date to the Chinese one.

This is not a straightforward procedure. However, there is some consolation in knowing that this first stage is perhaps the most arduous, and once this hurdle has been overcome, the remaining stages will seem easy by comparison.

Persevere, and on your first attempt you should complete this section in less than an hour. After that, practice and familiarity with the tables will speed up the process.

Worksheet No. 1 has been devised to help you through this complex stage. You may like to photocopy the worksheets in this book for your own use; alternatively, work on a piece of tracing paper which you can lay over them.

Adjustments to Time and Date of Birth

The Chinese Day begins with the First Double-Hour, which is reckoned from 11 p.m. the previous evening, so that midnight occurs at the mid-point of the first double-hour, and noon at the mid-point of the seventh double-hour. Because of this, birth-times between 11.01 p.m. (23.01) and midnight actually belong, in the Chinese calendar, to the following day. Of course, this may also affect the month, and even (in exceptional cases) the year of birth.

Daylight Saving Time, which may remove up to two hours from the birth-time, may have the same effect, but in reverse. Sometimes, however, these two adjustments (the Daylight Saving Time adjustment, and the final hour adjustment) may simply cancel each other out.

Worksheet 1 – How to Convert the Date

Objectives

1. To convert the date of birth to the Chinese date of birth.
2. To convert the Chinese date of birth to the Four Pillars.

Procedure

Note the time and date of birth.
Adjust the time of birth according to Daylight Saving Time if necessary.*
Adjust the date of birth if affected by the time of birth.
Evaluate the Chinese Hour of birth.
Evaluate the Chinese Year of birth.
Evaluate the Chinese Lunar Month of birth.
Evaluate the Day of the Chinese Lunar Month.
Evaluate the Stems and Branches for the Hour, Day, Month and Year of birth.

Method

Time and Date of Birth

STEP 1.   Enter the time of birth.   1≫

STEP 2.   Note whether there is any adjustment necessary for Daylight Saving Time.   2≫

STEP 3.   Enter the Corrected Time of Birth.   [ctb]≫

STEP 4.   From Table I, Table of Chinese Hours, note the Hour Branch pertaining to the Corrected Time of Birth.   [HB]≫

As explained in the opening section on the Stems and Branches, the convention adopted throughout this book is that branches are written as roman numerals.

STEP 5.   Enter date of birth.   5≫

STEP 6.   If the Corrected Time of Birth (STEP 3) is between 11.01 p.m. (23.01) and midnight, add one day to the date of birth.   [cdb]≫

The Day of Birth

STEPS 7, 8, 9 call for a leap-year adjustment if one is necessary. Before entering the required figure, add 1 for the leap-year adjustment if the Corrected Date of Birth falls on or after 29 February in a leap year.

No general rule as to the dates of Daylight Saving Time can be given, as they vary not only from year to year but from country to country. If in doubt, consult some standard reference work such as D. Chase Doane's *Time Changes in the World*, published by the American Federation of Astrologers, 1982.

STEP 7.   Refer to Table II. In the first column, find the Corrected Date of Birth. From Column A ('dcn'), find the Daily Code Number for the Corrected Date of Birth. Add 1 if there is a leap-year adjustment.   **Enter dcn (+1) [dcn]**≫

STEP 8.   From the same table (Table II), from column B ('dsc') note the Daily Stem Code. Add 1 if there is a leap-year adjustment.   **Enter dsc (+1) [dsc]**≫

STEP 9.   From the same table (Table II), from column C ('dbc') note the Daily Branch Code. Add 1 if there is a leap-year adjustment.   **Enter dbc (+1) [dbc]**≫

The Year of Birth

STEP 10.   Refer to Table III. Find the year of birth in the 'Western Year' column, and note the first monthly code number, in the column head NY. Enter this figure.   **NY**≫

If [NY] is less than, or equal to, the Daily Code Number [dcn], go to STEP 11.
   But if [NY] is greater than the Daily Code Number [dcn], go to STEP 12.

STEP 11.   Enter the Year of the Corrected Date of Birth as the Corrected Western Year (Omit STEP 12)   [cwy]≫

STEP 12.   Subtract 1 from the year of the Corrected Date of Birth, and enter this as the Corrected Western Year.   [cwy]≫

STEP 13.   From Table III, to the left of the Corrected Western Year, note the Yearly Code Number.   [ycn]≫

STEP 14.   From Table III, alongside the Corrected Western Year, note, from the second column from the right, the Year Stem.   [YS]≫

STEP 15.   From Table III, alongside the Corrected Western Year, note, from the extreme right-hand column, the Year Branch.
(As was the case with the Hour Branch, the Year Branch will be found written as a roman numeral.)   [YB]≫

STEP 16.   From Table IV, alongside the Corrected Western Year, note the Common Name for the relevant Chinese Year.   [CY]≫

Finding the Chinese Lunar Month

STEP 17.   Return to Table III.
Refer to the central block of this table, headed 'Monthly Codes'. Examine the line of figures alongside the Corrected Western Year, and find the number which is *equal to* or the *nearest below* the Daily Code Number (see STEP 7 [dcn]).

NB. *Always take the Monthly Code which is lower than the Daily Code Number, no matter how great the difference may be, nor how close the next higher number.*

Keep the position of this number in mind, while making a note of the number itself, which is the Monthly Code Number.   **[mcn]**≫

STEP 18.   Having already noted the position of the Monthly Code Number, refer to the *head* of the column in which the number appears, to find the Chinese Lunar Month.   **[LM]**≫

STEP 19.   Similarly, noting the position of the Monthly Code Number, refer to the *foot* of the column to find the Monthly Branch.   **[MB]**≫
(As with the Branch of the Hour and the Year, the Monthly Branch will be found expressed as a roman numeral.)

Finding the day of the Chinese lunar month

STEP 20.   Subtract the Monthly Code Number (STEP 17, [mcn]) from the Daily Code Number (STEP 7, [dcn]).
If the answer is 31 or greater, subtract 31.
Add 1.
The result is the Chinese Day of the Lunar Month.   **[CD]**≫

STEP 21.   Refer to:
STEP 20 [CD] for the *day* of the Chinese Month;
STEP 18 [LM] for the Chinese lunar *month*;
STEP 16 [CY] for the popular Chinese *year* name.

The Chinese date can now be expressed fully as:
the [CD] day of the [LM] month in the [CY] year.

Calculating the Stem and Branch for the Day

STEP 22.   Refer back to STEP 8 and note the Daily Stem Code [dsc].
Refer back to STEP 13 and note the Yearly Code Number [ycn].
Add [dsc] and [ycn].
Divide the answer by 10 and note the remainder (or 10, if there is no remainder).
The result is the Day Stem.   **[DS]**≫

STEP 23.   Refer back to STEP 9 and note the Daily Branch Code [dbc].
Add [dbc] and [ycn].
Divide the answer by 12 and note the remainder (or 12, if there is no remainder).
The result is the Day Branch.
(As before, express the Day Branch as a roman numeral.)   **[DB]**≫

Finding the Stems of the Hour and the Month

STEP 24.   Refer to Table V.
From the Hour Branch (STEP 4, [HB])
and the Day Stem (STEP 22, [DS])
read off the Hour Stem.   **[HS]**≫

STEP 25. Refer to Table VI.
From the Month Branch (STEP 19, [MB])
and the Year Stem (STEP 14, [YS])
read off the Month Stem.

STEP 26. The Stems and Branches for the Hour, Day, Month, and Year, will be found above, at the following steps:

Hour Stem [HS] STEP 24.   Hour Branch [HB] STEP 4.
Day Stem [DS] STEP 22.   Day Branch [DB] STEP 23.
Month Stem [MS] STEP 25.   Month Branch [MB] STEP 19.
Year Stem [YS] STEP 14.   Year Branch [YB] STEP 15.

The Four Pillars of Fate

The Four Pillars of Fate are the Hour, Day, Month and Year of Birth expressed as Stems and Branches. They are usually depicted prominently at the head of the Chinese horoscope in a grid, thus:

Hour Stem	Day Stem	Month Stem	Year Stem
Hour Branch	Day Branch	Month Branch	Year Branch

Supplementary Calculation Sheet

STEP 1. Enter Time of Birth

STEP 2. Adjustment for Daylight Saving Time

STEP 3. Corrected Time of Birth [ctb]

STEP 4. To Table I   Hour Branch   [HB]
Enter [HB] in Table of the Four Pillars at the end of this section

STEP 5. Enter Day of Month, Month and Year of Birth

If [ctb] is between 11 p.m. and midnight, add 1 to day

Adjust month and year if necessary

STEP 6. Enter Corrected Date of Birth   [cdb]

STEP 7. To Table II, column A   [(dcn)]
Leap year adjustment?   [(+1)]
Corrected Daily Code Number   [dcn]

STEP 8. To Table II, column B   [(dsc)]
Leap year adjustment   [(+1)]

Corrected Daily Stem Code [dsc] ☐

STEP 9. To Table II, column C [(dbc)]

Leap year adjustment? [(+1)]

Corrected Daily Branch Code [dbc] ☐

STEP 10. Enter year of birth from STEP 6 ☐

To Table III, column NY   Enter NY [NY] ☐

From STEP 7, enter [dcn] [dcn] ☐

If [NY] less than or equal to [dcn] go to STEP 11
If [NY] is more than [dcn]   go to STEP 12

STEP 11.   Enter the year of the corrected date of birth
            at STEP 13

STEP 12.   Subtract 1 from corrected year of birth.
            Enter this new figure as [cwy] at STEP 13

STEP 13. Enter [cwy] ☐

To Table III; Column 1   Enter ycn [ycn] ☐

STEP 14.   To Table III   Enter Year Stem [YS] ☐
           Enter [YS] in Table of the Four Pillars at the end of this section

STEP 15.   To Table III   Enter Year Branch [YB] ☐
           Enter [YB] in Table of the Four Pillars at the end of this section

STEP 16.   To Table IV   Enter common year name [CY]

☐ ☐

STEP 17.   To Table III: (central block of figures)
                          Enter Monthly Code Number [mcn] ☐

STEP 18.   To Table III, head of column
                          Enter Chinese Lunar Month [LM] ☐

STEP 19.   To Table III, foot of column
                          Enter Monthly Branch [MB] ☐
           Enter [MB] in Table of Four Pillars at the end of this section

STEP 20.   [dcn] − [mcn] ☐ ☐   [   ] ☐
           if [dcn] − [mcn] 31 or more, subtract 31   [(−31)] ☐
                                          Aad 1   [+1] *1*
           Chinese Day of Lunar Month   [CD]

☐ ☐   ☐

STEP 21.   The Chinese Date is [CD] day of [LM] month in [CY] year

STEP 22.   Enter [dsc]   [dsc] ☐
           Enter [ycn of Western (uncorrected) year]   [ycn] ☐
                          [dsc] + [ycn] =   [   ] ☐
                          Divide by 10 =   [   ] ☐
Remainder is Day Stem   [DS] ☐

           Enter [DS] in Table of the Four Pillars at the end of this section

STEP 23. Enter [dbc]   [dbc]
          Enter [ycn of Western (uncorrected) year]   [ycn]
                                [dbc] + [ycn] =   [   ]
                                    Divide by 12 =   [   ]

Remainder is Day Branch   [DB]
Enter [DB] in Table of the Four Pillars at the end of this section

STEP 24. To Table V. From [HB]/[DS] Read Hour Stem   [   ]   [HS]   [   ]

          Enter [HS] in Table of the Four Pillars at the end of this section

STEP 25. To Table VI. From [MB]/[YS] Read Month Stem   [   ]   [MS]   [   ]

          Enter [MS] in Table of the Four Pillars at the end of this section

STEP 26. Enter the Stem and Branch of Hour, Day, Month, Year.

Table of the Four Pillars

[HS]	[DS]	[MS]	[YS]
[HB]	[DB]	[MB]	[YB]

Table I: Table of Chinese Hours The Chinese divide the day into twelve double-hours, beginning at 11.01 p.m., so that midnight is the mid-point of the first double-hour, and noon the mid-point of the seventh double-hour. It follows that if the time of birth is between 11.01 p.m. and midnight, the date of birth should be adjusted to the following day. This of course may also affect the month and even the year of birth, for astrological calculations. See text, First Stage, STEPS 1–6.

The twelve double-hours are named after the Twelve Branches (for further explanation, see Introduction), which throughout this book are expressed as roman numerals.

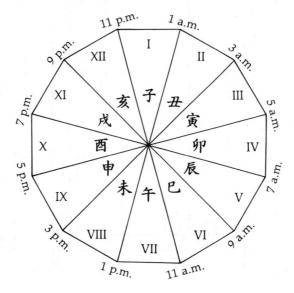

Table II: Daily Code Numbers This table gives daily codes for the purpose of calculating the Daily Stem, Branch, and Lunar Mansions, and actual Solar Mansions throughout the year. For explanations, see the relevant text.

Column A: Daily Code Number [dcn] (i.e., number of the day of the year).

Column B: Daily Stem Code [dsc] for calculating the Day Stem [DS]. For explanation, see First Stage, STEP 22, page 22.

Column C: Daily Branch Code [dbc] for calculating the Day Branch. See text, First Stage, STEP 23, page 22.

Column D: Lunar Mansion Code [lmc] for calculating the notional Lunar Mansion. See page 56.

Column E: Actual (approximate) positions of the Sun in the twenty-eight mansions throughout the year. For explanation, see page 60.

Important note: for Leap Years, add one day for all dates after and including 29 February

For all figures in the Table, add 1 for all dates after and including 29 February.

For example, for 31 December 1924, instead of:

31 Dec: 365 : 5 : 5 : 1 : 8

31 Dec: 366 : 6 : 6 : 2 : 9

	A	B	C	D	E		A	B	C	D	E		A	B	C	D	E
Jan 1	1	1	1	1	8	Feb 1	32	2	8	4	9	Mar 1	60	10	12	4	12
2	2	2	2	2	8	2	33	3	9	5	9	2	61	1	1	5	12
3	3	3	3	3	8	3	34	4	10	6	10	3	62	2	2	6	12
4	4	4	4	4	8	4	35	5	11	7	10	4	63	3	3	7	12
5	5	5	5	5	8	5	36	6	12	8	10	5	64	4	4	8	12
6	6	6	6	6	8	6	37	7	1	9	10	6	65	5	5	9	12
7	7	7	7	7	8	7	38	8	2	10	10	7	66	6	6	10	12
8	8	8	8	8	8	8	39	9	3	11	10	8	67	7	7	11	12
9	9	9	9	9	8	9	40	10	4	12	10	9	68	8	8	12	12
10	10	10	10	10	8	10	41	1	5	13	10	10	69	9	9	13	12
11	11	11	1	11	11	8	11	42	2	6	14	10	11	70	10	10	14	13
12	12	12	2	12	12	8	12	43	3	7	15	10	12	71	1	11	15	13
13	13	13	3	1	13	8	13	44	4	8	16	10	13	72	2	12	16	13
14	14	14	4	2	14	8	14	45	5	9	17	11	14	73	3	1	17	13
15	15	15	5	3	15	8	15	46	6	10	18	11	15	74	4	2	18	13
16	16	16	6	4	16	8	16	47	7	11	19	11	16	75	5	3	19	13
17	17	17	7	5	17	8	17	48	8	12	20	11	17	76	6	4	20	13
18	18	18	8	6	18	8	18	49	9	1	21	11	18	77	7	5	21	13
19	19	19	9	7	19	8	19	50	10	2	22	11	19	78	8	6	22	13
20	20	20	10	8	20	8	20	51	1	3	23	11	20	79	9	7	23	13
21	21	21	1	9	21	8	21	52	2	4	24	11	21	80	10	8	24	14
22	22	22	2	10	22	8	22	53	3	5	25	11	22	81	1	9	25	13
23	23	23	3	11	23	8	23	54	4	6	26	11	23	82	2	10	26	13
24	24	24	4	12	24	8	24	55	5	7	27	12	24	83	3	11	27	13
25	25	25	5	1	25	8	25	56	6	8	28	12	25	84	4	12	28	13
26	26	26	6	2	26	9	26	57	7	9	1	12	26	85	5	1	1	14
27	27	27	7	3	27	9	27	58	8	10	2	12	27	86	6	2	2	14
28	28	28	8	4	28	9	28	59	9	11	3	12	28	87	7	3	3	14
29	29	29	9	5	1	9	(29)						29	88	8	4	4	14
30	30	30	10	6	2	9							30	89	9	5	5	14
31	31	31	1	7	3	9							31	90	10	6	6	14

	A	B	C	D	E
Apr 1	91	1	7	7	14
2	92	2	8	8	14
3	93	3	9	9	14
4	94	4	10	10	14
5	95	5	11	11	14
6	96	6	12	12	14
7	97	7	1	13	14
8	98	8	2	14	14
9	99	9	3	15	14
10	100	10	4	16	14
11	101	1	5	17	14
12	102	2	6	18	14
13	103	3	7	19	14
14	104	4	8	20	15
15	105	5	9	21	15
16	106	6	10	22	15
17	107	7	11	23	15
18	108	8	12	24	16
19	109	9	1	25	16
20	110	10	2	26	16
21	111	1	3	27	16
22	112	2	4	28	16
23	113	3	5	1	16
24	114	4	6	2	16
25	115	5	7	3	16
26	116	6	8	4	16
27	117	7	9	5	16
28	118	8	10	6	17
29	119	9	11	7	17
30	120	10	12	8	17

	A	B	C	D	E
May 1	121	1	1	9	17
2	122	2	2	10	17
3	123	3	3	11	17
4	124	4	4	12	17
5	125	5	5	13	17
6	126	6	6	14	17
7	127	7	7	15	17
8	128	8	8	16	17
9	129	9	9	17	17
10	130	10	10	18	17
11	131	1	11	19	17
12	132	2	12	20	18
13	133	3	1	21	18
14	134	4	2	22	18
15	135	5	3	23	18
16	136	6	4	24	18
17	137	7	5	25	18
18	138	8	6	26	18
19	139	9	7	27	18
20	140	10	8	28	18
21	141	1	9	1	18
22	142	2	10	2	18
23	143	3	11	3	18
24	144	4	12	4	18
25	145	5	1	5	19
26	146	6	2	6	19
27	147	7	3	7	19
28	148	8	4	8	19
29	149	9	5	9	19
30	150	10	6	10	19
31	151	1	7	11	19

	A	B	C	D	E
Jun 1	152	2	8	12	19
2	153	3	9	13	19
3	154	4	10	14	19
4	155	5	11	15	19
5	156	6	12	16	19
6	157	7	1	17	19
7	158	8	2	18	19
8	159	9	3	19	19
9	160	10	4	20	19
10	161	1	5	21	19
11	162	2	6	22	19
12	163	3	7	23	19
13	164	4	8	24	20
14	165	5	9	25	20
15	166	6	10	26	20
16	167	7	11	27	20
17	168	8	12	28	20
18	169	9	1	1	20
19	170	10	2	2	21
20	171	1	3	3	21
21	172	2	4	4	21
22	173	3	5	5	21
23	174	4	6	6	21
24	175	5	7	7	21
25	176	6	8	8	21
26	177	7	9	9	22
27	178	8	10	10	22
28	179	9	11	11	22
29	180	10	12	12	22
30	181	1	1	13	22

	A	B	C	D	E
Jul 1	182	2	2	14	22
2	183	3	3	15	22
3	184	4	4	16	22
4	185	5	5	17	22
5	186	6	6	18	22
6	187	7	7	19	22
7	188	8	8	20	22
8	189	9	9	21	22
9	190	10	10	22	22
10	191	1	11	23	22
11	192	2	12	24	22
12	193	3	1	25	22
13	194	4	2	26	22
14	195	5	3	27	22
15	196	6	4	28	22
16	197	7	5	1	22
17	198	8	6	2	22
18	199	9	7	3	22
19	200	10	8	4	22
20	201	1	9	5	22
21	202	2	10	6	22
22	203	3	11	7	22
23	204	4	12	8	22
24	205	5	1	9	22
25	206	6	2	10	22
26	207	7	3	11	22
27	208	8	4	12	22
28	209	9	5	13	22
29	210	10	6	14	22
30	211	1	7	15	22
31	212	2	8	16	22

	A	B	C	D	E
Aug 1	213	3	9	17	23
2	214	4	10	18	23
3	215	5	11	19	23
4	216	6	12	20	23
5	217	7	1	21	24
6	218	8	2	22	24
7	219	9	3	23	24
8	220	10	4	24	24
9	221	1	5	25	24
10	222	2	6	26	24
11	223	3	7	27	24
12	224	4	8	28	24
13	225	5	9	1	24
14	226	6	10	2	24
15	227	7	11	3	24
16	228	8	12	4	24
17	229	9	1	5	24
18	230	10	2	6	24
19	231	1	3	7	24
20	232	2	4	8	25
21	233	3	5	9	25
22	234	4	6	10	25
23	235	5	7	11	25
24	236	6	8	12	25
25	237	7	9	13	25
26	238	8	10	14	25
27	239	9	11	15	25
28	240	10	12	16	26
29	241	1	1	17	26
30	242	2	2	18	26
31	243	3	3	19	26

	A	B	C	D	E
Sep 1	244	4	4	20	26
2	245	5	5	21	26
3	246	6	6	22	26
4	247	7	7	23	26
5	248	8	8	24	26
6	249	9	9	25	26
7	250	10	10	26	26
8	251	1	11	27	26
9	252	2	12	28	26
10	253	3	1	1	26
11	254	4	2	2	26
12	255	5	3	3	26
13	256	6	4	4	27
14	257	7	5	5	27
15	258	8	6	6	27
16	259	9	7	7	27
17	260	10	8	8	27
18	261	1	9	9	27
19	262	2	10	10	27
20	263	3	11	11	27
21	264	4	12	12	27
22	265	5	1	13	27
23	266	6	2	14	27
24	267	7	3	15	27
25	268	8	4	16	27
26	269	9	5	17	27
27	270	10	6	18	27
28	271	1	7	19	27
29	272	2	8	20	28
30	273	3	9	21	28

	A	B	C	D	E
Oct 1	274	4	10	22	28
2	275	5	11	23	28
3	276	6	12	24	28
4	277	7	1	25	28
5	278	8	2	26	28
6	279	9	3	27	28
7	280	10	4	28	28
8	281	1	5	1	28
9	282	2	6	2	28
10	283	3	7	3	28
11	284	4	8	4	28
12	285	5	9	5	28
13	286	6	10	6	28
14	287	7	11	7	28
15	288	8	12	8	1
16	289	9	1	9	1
17	290	10	2	10	1
18	291	1	3	11	1
19	292	2	4	12	1
20	293	3	5	13	1
21	294	4	6	14	1
22	295	5	7	15	1
23	296	6	8	16	1
24	297	7	9	17	1
25	298	8	10	18	1
26	299	9	11	19	2
27	300	10	12	20	2
28	301	1	1	21	2
29	302	2	2	22	2
30	303	3	3	23	2
31	304	4	4	24	2

	A	B	C	D	E
Nov 1	305	5	5	25	2
2	306	6	6	26	2
3	307	7	7	27	3
4	308	8	8	28	3
5	309	9	9	1	3
6	310	10	10	2	3
7	311	1	11	3	3
8	312	2	12	4	3
9	313	3	1	5	3
10	314	4	2	6	3
11	315	5	3	7	3
12	316	6	4	8	3
13	317	7	5	9	3
14	318	8	6	10	3
15	319	9	7	11	3
16	320	10	8	12	3
17	321	1	9	13	3
18	322	2	10	14	3
19	323	3	11	15	4
20	324	4	12	16	4
21	325	5	1	17	4
22	326	6	2	18	4
23	327	7	3	19	5
24	328	8	4	20	5
25	329	9	5	21	5
26	330	10	6	22	5
27	331	1	7	23	5
28	332	2	8	24	6
29	333	3	9	25	6
30	334	4	10	26	6

	A	B	C	D	E
Dec 1	335	5	11	27	6
2	336	6	12	28	6
3	337	7	1	1	6
4	338	8	2	2	6
5	339	9	3	3	6
6	340	10	4	4	6
7	341	1	5	5	6
8	342	2	6	6	6
9	343	3	7	7	6
10	344	4	8	8	6
11	345	5	9	9	6
12	346	6	10	10	6
13	347	7	11	11	6
14	348	8	12	12	6
15	349	9	1	13	6
16	350	10	2	14	6
17	351	1	3	15	6
18	352	2	4	16	7
19	353	3	5	17	7
20	354	4	6	18	7
21	355	5	7	19	7
22	356	6	8	20	7
23	357	7	9	21	7
24	358	8	10	22	7
25	359	9	11	23	7
26	360	10	12	24	7
27	361	1	1	25	7
28	362	2	2	26	7
29	363	3	3	27	7
30	364	4	4	28	8
31	365	5	5	1	8

Table III: Code Numbers for Calculating the Chinese Lunar Date (see Worksheet 1)

Chinese Months — Monthly Codes

Yearly Code	WESTERN YEAR (NY)	1st	2nd	3rd	4th	5th	6th	7th	8th	9th	10th	11th	12th	Year Stem	Year Branch
15	1901	50	79	109	138	167	197	226	256	285	315	345 1	10	8	II
20	1902	39	69	98	128	157	186	216	245	275	304	334	364 1	9	III
25	1903	29	58	88	117	147	205	235	264	293	323	353 1	17	10	IV
30	1904	47	76	106	135	165	194	223	253	282	311	341 1	6	1	V
36	1905	35	65	95	124	154	184	213	242	272	301	331	360 1	2	VI
41	1906	25	54	84	114	173	202	232	261	291	320	350 1	14	3	VII
46	1907	44	73	104	132	162	191	221	251	280	310	339 1	4	4	VIII
51	1908	33	62	91	120	150	180	209	239	268	298	328	357 1	5	IX
57	1909	22	51	110	139	169	198	228	257	287	317	347 1	11	6	X
2	1910	41	70	100	129	158	188	217	247	276	306	336	1	7	XI
7	1911	30	60	89	119	148	177	236	265	295	325	354 1	19	8	XII
12	1912	49	78	107	137	166	195	225	254	283	313	343 1	7	9	I
18	1913	47	67	97	126	156	185	214	244	273	302	332	361 1	10	II
23	1914	26	56	86	115	145	204	233	263	292	322	351 1	15	1	III
28	1915	45	75	104	134	164	193	223	252	282	311	341 1	5	2	IV
33	1916	34	63	93	122	152	181	211	242	270	300	329	359 1	3	V
39	1917	23	53	111	141	170	200	230	259	289	319	348 1	13	4	VI
44	1918	42	72	101	130	160	189	219	248	278	308	337 1	2	5	VII
49	1919	32	61	91	120	149	179	208	267	297	326	356 1	21	6	VIII
54	1920	51	79	109	138	167	197	226	255	285	315	344 1	9	7	IX

Monthly Branch (under months 1st–12th): III IV V VI VII VIII IX X XI XII I II

Yearly Code	WESTERN YEAR	1st	2nd	3rd	4th	5th	6th	7th	8th	9th	10th	11th		12th		Year Stem	Year Branch
0	1921	39	69	98	128	157	186	216	245	274	304	333		363	1	8	X
5	1922	28	58	87	117	147	205	235	264	293	323	352	1	17		9	XI
10	1923	47	76	106	136	165	195	224	254	283	312	342	1	6		10	XII
15	1924	36	65	94	124	153	183	213	242	272	301	331		360	1	1	I
21	1925	25	54	83	113	172	202	231	261	291	320	350	1	14		2	II
26	1926	44	73	102	132	161	191	220	250	280	309	339	1	4		3	III
31	1927	33	63	92	121	151	180	210	239	269	299	328		358	1	4	IV
36	1928	23	52	110	139	169	198	227	257	286	316	346	1	11		5	V
42	1929	41	70	100	129	158	188	217	246	276	305	335		365	1	6	VI
47	1930	30	59	89	119	148	177	236	265	295	324	354	1	19		7	VII
52	1931	48	78	108	137	167	196	226	255	284	314	343	1	8		8	VIII
57	1932	37	66	96	126	155	185	214	244	273	302	332		361	1	9	IX
3	1933	26	55	85	195	144	204	233	263	292	322	351	1	15		10	X
8	1934	45	74	104	133	163	193	222	252	281	311	341	1	5		1	XI
13	1935	35	64	93	123	152	182	211	241	271	300	330		360	1	2	XII
18	1936	24	54	82	141	170	199	229	259	288	318	348	1	13		3	I
24	1937	42	72	101	130	160	189	218	248	277	307	337	1	2		4	II
29	1938	31	61	91	120	149	179	208	267	296	326	355	1	20		5	III
34	1939	50	80	110	139	168	198	227	256	286	315	345	1	9		6	IV
39	1940	39	68	98	127	157	186	216	245	274	304	333		363	1	7	V
45	1941	27	57	87	116	146	176	235	264	293	323	352	1	17		8	VI
50	1942	46	76	105	135	165	194	224	253	283	312	342	1	6		9	VII
55	1943	36	65	95	124	154	183	213	243	272	302	331		361	1	10	VIII
0	1944	25	55	83	113	172	201	231	260	290	320	349	1	14		1	IX
6	1945	44	73	102	132	161	190	220	249	279	309	339	1	3		2	X
11	1946	33	63	92	121	151	180	209	239	268	298	328		357	1	3	XI
16	1947	22	52	111	140	170	199	228	258	287	317	346	1	11		4	XII
21	1948	41	70	99	129	158	188	217	246	276	305	335		364	1	5	I
27	1949	29	59	88	118	148	177	207	234	265	295	354	1	18		6	II
32	1950	48	77	107	137	166	196	226	255	284	314	343	1	8		7	III
37	1951	37	67	96	126	156	185	215	244	274	303	333		362	1	8	IV
42	1952	27	56	85	114	144	203	232	262	292	321	351	1	15		9	V
48	1953	45	74	104	133	162	192	221	251	281	311	340	1	5		10	VI
53	1954	35	64	94	123	152	181	211	240	270	300	329		359	1	1	VII
58	1955	24	53	83	142	171	200	230	259	289	318	348	1	13		2	VIII
3	1956	43	71	101	130	160	189	218	248	277	300	336			1	3	IX
9	1957	31	61	90	120	149	179	208	237	296	326	355	1	20		4	X
14	1958	49	79	109	139	168	198	227	256	286	315	345	1	9		5	XI
19	1959	39	68	98	128	157	187	216	246	275	305	335		364	1	6	XII
24	1960	28	58	86	116	145	175	234	264	293	323	352	1	17		7	I
30	1961	46	76	105	135	164	194	223	253	283	312	343	1	6		8	II
35	1962	36	65	95	124	153	183	212	242	272	301	331		361	1	9	III
40	1963	25	55	84	114	172	202	231	261	290	320	350	1	15		10	IV
45	1964	44	73	102	132	161	190	220	249	279	308	338	1	3		1	V
51	1965	13	62	92	121	151	180	209	239	268	297	327		357	1	2	VI
56	1966	21	51	81	140	170	199	228	258	287	316	346	1	11		3	VII
1	1967	40	70	100	129	159	189	218	247	277	306	336		365	1	4	VIII
6	1968	30	59	88	117	147	177	206	265	295	326	354	1	18		5	IX
12	1969	48	77	107	136	166	195	225	255	284	314	343	1	8		6	X
17	1970	37	67	96	125	155	184	214	244	273	303	333		362	1	7	XI
22	1971	27	56	86	115	144	203	233	262	292	322	352	1	16		8	XII
27	1972	46	74	104	133	162	192	221	251	280	310	340	1	4		9	I
33	1973	34	64	93	123	152	181	211	240	269	299	329		358	1	10	II
38	1974	23	53	83	112	171	200	230	259	288	318	348	1	12		1	III
43	1975	42	72	102	131	161	190	219	249	278	307	337			1	2	IV
48	1976	31	60	90	119	149	178	208	237	296	325	355	1	19		3	V
54	1977	49	79	108	138	168	197	227	256	286	315	345	1	9		4	VI
59	1978	38	68	97	127	157	186	216	245	275	305	334		364	1	5	VII
4	1979	28	58	87	116	146	175	235	264	294	324	353	1	18		6	VIII
9	1980	47	76	105	134	164	193	223	252	282	312	341	1	6		7	IX
15	1981	36	65	95	124	153	183	212	241	271	301	330		360	1	8	X
20	1982	25	55	84	114	172	202	231	260	290	319	349	1	14		9	XI

Monthly Branch: III | IV | V | VI | VII | VIII | IX | X | XI | XII | I | II

Yearly Code	WESTERN YEAR	1st (NY)	2nd	3rd	4th	5th	6th	7th	8th	9th	10th	11th	12th	Year Stem	Year Branch
25	1983	44	74	103	133	162	191	221	250	279	309	338 1	3	10	XII
30	1984	33	62	91	121	151	180	209	239	268	297	356 1	21	1	I
36	1985	51	80	110	140	169	199	228	258	287	316	346 1	10	2	II
41	1986	40	69	99	129	158	188	219	247	277	306	336	365 1	3	III
46	1987	29	59	88	118	147	177	236	266	296	325	355 1	19	4	IV
51	1988	48	77	106	136	165	195	224	254	284	313	343 1	8	5	V
57	1989	37	67	96	125	155	184	213	243	273	302	332	362 1	6	VI
2	1990	27	56	86	115	144	203	232	262	291	321	351 1	16	7	VII
7	1991	46	75	105	134	163	193	222	251	281	310	340 1	5	8	VIII
12	1992	35	63	93	123	152	181	211	240	269	299	328	358 1	9	IX
18	1993	23	52	82	141	171	200	230	259	288	318	347 1	12	10	X
23	1994	41	71	101	131	160	190	219	249	278	307	337	1	1	XI
28	1995	31	60	90	120	149	179	208	238	297	326	356 1	20	2	XII
33	1996	50	78	108	137	167	197	226	256	285	315	345 1	9	3	I
39	1997	38	68	97	127	156	186	215	245	275	304	334	364 1	4	II
44	1998	28	58	87	116	146	204	234	264	293	323	353 1	17	5	III
49	1999	47	77	106	135	165	194	223	253	282	312	342 1	7	6	IV
54	2000	36	65	95	124	153	183	212	241	271	300	330	360 1	7	V

Chinese Months — Monthly Codes

Monthly Branch: III IV V VI VII VIII IX X XI XII I II

Table IV: *Common Names for the Chinese Years* The following animal-element names are the ones by which the years are usually known in Tibet, Mongolia and other parts of Asia. The left-hand column gives the approximate corresponding Western calendar year or 'Corrected Western Year' [cwy]. For further details, see First Stage, STEPS 10ff.

1900	Metal-Rat	1920	Metal-Monkey	1940	Metal-Dragon
1901	Metal-Ox	1921	Metal-Cockerel	1941	Metal-Snake
1902	Water-Tiger	1922	Water-Dog	1942	Water-Horse
1903	Water-Rabbit	1923	Water-Pig	1943	Water-Sheep
1904	Wood-Dragon	1924	Wood-Rat	1944	Wood-Monkey
1905	Wood-Snake	1925	Wood-Ox	1945	Wood-Cockerel
1906	Fire-Horse	1926	Fire-Tiger	1946	Fire-Dog
1907	Fire-Sheep	1927	Fire-Rabbit	1947	Fire-Pig
1908	Earth-Monkey	1928	Earth-Dragon	1948	Earth-Rat
1909	Earth-Cockerel	1929	Earth-Snake	1949	Earth-Ox
1910	Metal-Dog	1930	Metal-Horse	1950	Metal-Tiger
1911	Metal-Pig	1931	Metal-Sheep	1951	Metal-Rabbit
1912	Water-Rat	1932	Water-Monkey	1952	Water-Dragon
1913	Water-Ox	1933	Water-Cockerel	1953	Water-Snake
1914	Wood-Tiger	1934	Wood-Dog	1954	Wood-Horse
1915	Wood-Rabbit	1935	Wood-Pig	1955	Wood-Sheep
1916	Fire-Dragon	1936	Fire-Rat	1956	Fire-Monkey
1917	Fire-Snake	1937	Fire-Ox	1957	Fire-Cockerel
1918	Earth-Horse	1938	Earth-Tiger	1958	Earth-Dog
1919	Earth-Sheep	1939	Earth-Rabbit	1959	Earth-Pig

1960	Metal-Rat	1974	Wood-Tiger	1988	Earth-Dragon
1961	Metal-Ox	1975	Wood-Rabbit	1989	Earth-Snake
1962	Water-Tiger	1976	Fire-Dragon	1990	Metal-Horse
1963	Water-Rabbit	1977	Fire-Snake	1991	Metal-Sheep
1964	Wood-Dragon	1978	Earth-Horse	1992	Water-Monkey
1965	Wood-Snake	1979	Earth-Sheep	1993	Water-Cockerel
1966	Fire-Horse	1980	Metal-Monkey	1994	Wood-Dog
1967	Fire-Sheep	1981	Metal-Cockerel	1995	Wood-Pig
1968	Earth-Monkey	1982	Water-Dog	1996	Fire-Rat
1969	Earth-Cockerel	1983	Water-Pig	1997	Fire-Ox
1970	Metal-Dog	1984	Wood-Rat	1998	Earth-Tiger
1971	Metal-Pig	1985	Wood-Ox	1999	Earth-Rabbit
1972	Water-Rat	1986	Fire-Tiger	2000	Metal-Dragon
1973	Water-Ox	1987	Fire-Rabbit		

Table V: Table to find the Stem of the Hour. For explanation, see First Stage, STEP 24.

Hour Branch [HB]

Day Stem	I	II	III	IV	V	VI	VII	VIII	IX	X	XI	XII
1 or 6	1	2	3	4	5	6	7	8	9	10	1	2
2 or 7	3	4	5	6	7	8	9	10	1	2	3	4
3 or 8	5	6	7	8	9	10	1	2	3	4	6	6
4 or 9	7	8	9	10	1	2	3	4	5	6	7	8
5 or 10	9	10	1	2	3	4	5	6	7	8	9	10

Table VI: Table to find the Stem of the Month. For explanation, see First Stage, STEP 25.

Month Branch [MB]

Year Stem	I	II	III	IV	V	VI	VII	VIII	IX	X	XI	XII
1 or 6	3	4	5	6	7	8	9	10	1	2	3	4
2 or 7	5	6	7	8	9	10	1	2	3	4	5	6
3 or 8	7	8	9	10	1	2	3	4	5	6	7	8
4 or 9	9	10	1	2	3	4	5	6	7	8	9	10
5 or 10	1	2	3	4	5	6	7	8	9	10	1	2

The Twelve Regions

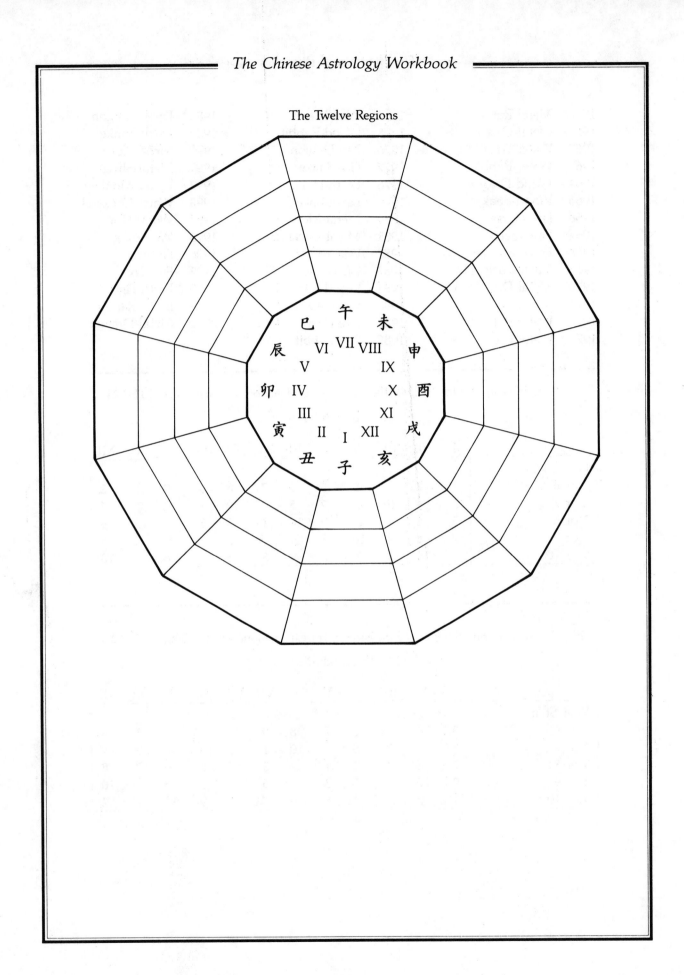

3.

The Rulers of the Purple Palace or Great Bear Astrology

Introduction

Now that the Four Pillars have been calculated, it is possible to turn to an important system of Chinese astrology known as the Tzu Wei (in Cantonese pronounced *cheeway*), or Purple Crepe Myrtle, method. This traces one's fate through influences of the principal and neighbouring stars of the constellation of the Great Bear, which is believed to be the residence of the Purple Crepe Myrtle Genie. Purple is the Imperial colour, and also the colour associated with the Central Palace of the Heavens, which includes the Great Bear constellation, known to the Chinese as the Northern Ladle.

Though it is the most brilliant of the constellations of the Northern Palace, the most important stars, as far as Chinese astrologers are concerned, are those which are closest to the Pole Star, since this represents the Emperor, and the stars closest to it the Emperor's courtiers and advisers.

The planet associated with the Central Palace is Jupiter, the Wood Star, while the imaginary planet Counter-Jupiter, the Reckoner of Years, is regarded as the abode of the Minister of Time, revered in several temples dedicated to him throughout the Far East as the judge of one's destiny.

Purple Crepe Myrtle astrology is concerned only with the fixed stars, not the motions of the planets, since it is believed that even these are subject to the edicts of the Minister of Time – as indeed, in a practical sense, they are. There are several books in Chinese on the subject of Purple Crepe Myrtle astrology, but they vary considerably in the number and names of the stars which they involve, and even in the methods of calculating the influences of the stars.

I have researched all the available methods, noting particularly the points on which they are all in agreement. Then, for complete authenticity, these have been compared with the most ancient available texts on the subject, enshrined in the Taoist Sacred Classics.* These essays, compiled in the eighth and ninth centuries, are highly sophisticated in their detailed treatment of the Purple Crepe Myrtle astrological method, thus revealing

---

*Source: *Tao Tsang*, Vol. 1, 114, section 1474.

that it must have been both highly organized and well-established by that period. Indeed, from scattered hints in the established classics, as well as tangible evidence of the discovery of actual astrological instruments of the period, it seems that Purple Crepe Myrtle astrology must have been flourishing by the first century BC at least.

In this section, we can see the Chinese horoscope beginning to emerge.

The shape which has been adopted here for compiling the horoscope charts is the twelve-sided figure, or 'spider's web' shape of the Yuan Dynasty (thirteenth century). Strictly speaking, this is not the traditional shape for the Tzu Wei horoscope. To judge from available evidence, the earliest Chinese horoscope charts were probably segmented squares (see below) while the traditional shape for the Tzu Wei horoscope is an oblong. After the 'spider's web' shape came the segmented circle, used at present for charts in the West. Curiously enough, the Chinese then adopted the Indian pattern at about the same time that in the West, the Indian shape was being abandoned in favour of the 'modern' segmented circle.

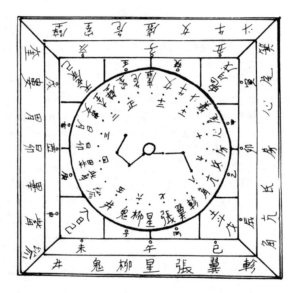

Early Han Diviner's Instrument

The unusual name of the tutelary genius of Great Bear Astrology, Tzu Wei, the Purple Crepe Myrtle Genie, may possibly be derived from the first rule in the method, which relates to the Earthly Branches Tzu (Branch I) and Wei (Branch VIII), although the Chinese characters for these words are completely distinctive.

Basic Principles

One of the principles of Purple Crepe Myrtle astrology is that the stars of the Purple Palace – that is, the area of the sky closest to the Celestial Pole, rule those regions of the sky which border upon it. Each of the stars has certain attributes – good or bad – which influence the respective divisions of the sky.

As the Earth progresses through the heavens, and any location on its surface passes underneath each of these regions in turn, so the destinies of the persons born there at that moment in time are governed by the deities which rule those regions.

(a) The Twelve Regions

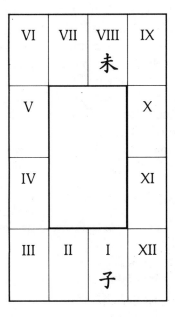

As there must be a starting-point to which all other calculations refer, the twelve divisions of the 'spider's web' horoscope chart represent the twelve regions.

These twelve regions are traditionally marked by the Twelve Branches, and commence with Tzu (Branch I) at the bottom. The other eleven regions follow in clockwise order.

The position of the Twelve Regions *is invariable*.

(b) The Twelve Principal Stars

The names of the twelve principal stars of Purple Crepe Myrtle astrology are as follows.:

a	Tzu Wei	The Purple Crepe Myrtle
b	T'ien Hsü	Heaven's Void
c	T'ien Kuei	Heaven's Honour
d	T'ien Yin	Heaven's Seal
e	T'ien Shou	Heaven's Longevity
f	T'ien K'ung	Heaven's Space
g	Hung Luan	The Red Phoenix
h	T'ien K'u	Heaven's Granary
i	T'ien Kuan	Heaven's Money
j	Wen Ch'ang	Literary Excellence
k	T'ien Fu	Heaven's Fortune
l	T'ien Lu	Heaven's Reward

(c) Assigning the Twelve Chief Stars

The positions, or Palaces, of the twelve principal stars on the horoscope plate is determined by the Palace of the first star, the Purple Crepe Myrtle Star, Tzu Wei itself.

First, refer to the Four Pillars (from the preceding chapter) to find the Branch of the year of birth.

Then, beginning at the region marked Wei (Branch VIII) and counting that region as Tzu (Branch I) number off each region until you arrive at the Branch of the year of birth. That Palace is the Purple Crepe Myrtle Palace.

(For example, suppose that the Branch of the Year of Birth is Shen (Branch IX); then beginning with Branch I (Tzu) in the Eighth (Wei) Region, and counting up to (IX) Shen, you arrive at the Fourth (Mao) Region. Thus, for a birth year branch IX (Shen), the Purple Crepe Myrtle Palace will be Mao.

The twelve palaces of the chief stars are then positioned in *anticlockwise* order round the twelve regions.

(d) The Seven Auxiliary Stars

In addition to the twelve principal stars, there are other less significant stars which help to determine the destiny. These are called:

m	T'ien Chang	Heaven's Staff
n	T'ien I	Heaven's Curiosity
o	Mao T'ou	Hair and Fur
p	T'ien Jen	Heaven's Axe
q	T'ien Hsing	Heaven's Punishment
r	T'ien Yang	Heaven's Elegance
s	T'ien K'u	Heaven's Lamenting

Rules to find the Position of Auxiliary Stars

With the exception of Star *s, T'ien K'u, Heaven's Lamenting, the positions of the auxiliary stars are all derived from the *month* of birth.

The following are the basic rules to find the positions of stars *m, *n, *o, and *p, T'ien Chang, Heaven's Staff, T'ien I, Heaven's Curiosity, Mao T'ou, Hair and Fur, and T'ien Jen, Heaven's Axe.

From the preceding section, note the Chinese Lunar Month of birth (STEP 18, [LM]). Then count out anti-clockwise from the First Region, until you arrive at the region corresponding to the number of the Lunar Month.

Example: commencing at the Tzu (I) Region, count out the regions in anti-clockwise order up to nine (for the ninth month). You finish at Region V. This fixes the position of Star *m T'ien Chang.

The other three auxiliary stars *n, *o, and *p, occupy the regions following the T'ien Chang in anticlockwise order round the chart.

Other rules, however, dictate the positions of the remaining stars. The rules are given here for the sake of completeness, although the basic information is given in a table at the end of this section.

Rule to find Star *q T'ien Hsing, Heaven's Punishment
Count out the number of months to the birth month, commencing at the Yu (X) Region, but count in *clockwise* order.

Rule to find Star *r T'ien Yang, Heaven's Elegance
Count out the number of months to the birth month, commencing at the Chou (II) Region, again in clockwise order.

Rule to find Star *s T'ien K'u, Heaven's Lamenting
Unlike the other auxiliary stars, the Star *s, T'ien Ku, is found from the branch of the birth *year*.
Count out to the branch of the birth year, in an anticlockwise direction, commencing at the Chou (II) Region.

Fortunate and Unfortunate Stars

The Nineteen Stars are classed as Fortunate or Unfortunate. There are nine fortunate stars (marked [f] in the table below), nine unfortunate stars (marked [u]), and one which is sometimes fortunate and sometimes unfortunate — *i, T'ien Kuan, Heaven's Money.

Table VII

a	Tzu Wei	The Purple Crepe Myrtle	f	+
b	T'ien Hsü	Heaven's Emptiness	u	−
c	T'ien Kuei	Heaven's Honour	f	−
d	T'ien Yin	Heaven's Seal	f	+
e	T'ien Shou	Heaven's Longevity	f	+
f	T'ien K'ung	Heaven's Space	u	*
g	Hung Luan	The Red Phoenix	f	−
h	T'ien K'u	Heaven's Granary	f	+
i	T'ien Kuan	Heaven's Money	*	−
j	Wen Ch'ang	Literary Excellence	f	+
k	T'ien Fu	Heaven's Fortune	f	+
l	T'ien Lu	Heaven's Reward	f	+
m	T'ien Chang	Heaven's Staff	u	+
n	T'ien I	Heaven's Curiosity	u	−
o	Mao T'ou	Hair and Fur	u	−
p	T'ien Jen	Heaven's Axe	u	−
q	T'ien Hsing	Heaven's Punishment	u	−
r	T'ien Yang	Heaven's Elegance	u	+
s	T'ien K'u	Heaven's Lamenting	u	−

The Yin and Yang Palaces

The Nineteen stars are also considered to be either yin or yang. The nine yang (positive) stars are those marked [+] and the nine yin stars are those marked [−] in the table above. There is also one star, T'ien K'ung, Heaven's Space, which is neither yin nor yang.

Similarly the twelve regions are also considered yin or yang, but do not follow the usual rule that the odd-numbered branches are yang, and the even-numbered branches yin. Instead, the yang regions are considered to be those designated by the branches IV (Mao), V (Chen), VI (Ssu), VII (Wu), VIII (Wei), and IX (Shen). Conversely, the yin regions are: X (Yu), XI (Hsu), XII (Hai), I (Tzu), II (Chou), and III (Yin).

When the yin or yang stars are positioned in their own type of region (a yang star sits in a yang region, or a yin star sits in a yin region), then one may conclude that good fortune will be in abundance, and misfortunes slight. But if a region is occupied by a star of the opposite type (a yang star sits in a yin region, or a yin star sits in a yang region), then good fortune will be slight, and calamities great.

The Temple, Radiance and Pleasure

When a star sits in its most suited region, this is termed Miao, 'The Temple'. When it sits in the second-most suited region, this is termed Wang, 'Radiance', and when in its third-most suited region, Lo, meaning 'Pleasure'. But if they are in a region to which they are not suited, this is called Shih Hsien, 'Falling to the Enemy'.

The Temple, Radiance and Pleasure pertaining to each star are shown in Table VIII.

Table VIII: The Twelve Regions and the Stars

	Star	Temple	Radiance	Pleasure
a	PURPLE CREPE MYRTLE	VI, X	I	IX, XII
b	HEAVEN'S VOID	VII	II	–
c	HEAVEN'S HONOUR	V	XII	III
d	HEAVEN'S SEAL	I	IV, V	XII
e	HEAVEN'S LONGEVITY	XII	X	III
f	HEAVEN'S SPACE	–	–	–
g	RED PHOENIX	II, XII	–	V, III
h	HEAVEN'S GRANARY	VII	XII, VI	IV, VIII
i	HEAVEN'S MONEY	IV, VIII	VI, XII	V, VII
j	LITERARY EXCELLENCE	III, XI	VII	–
k	HEAVEN'S FORTUNE	IV	III	VI
l	HEAVEN'S REWARD	IX	VI	IV
m	Heaven's Staff	–	I, VII, IX, XII	–
n	Heaven's Curiosity	II, VII	–	V
o	Hair and Fur	III	I, IV	VII, XI
p	Heaven's Axe	VI, IX	VII, X	III
q	Heaven's Punishment	III, XI	X	VII
r	Heaven's Elegance	IV, XI	V	XII
s	Heaven's Lamenting	II, IX	IV, V	–

Table IX displays the Temple, Radiance, Pleasure, and Falling to the Enemy for each star in each of the Twelve regions.

>T< : Temple   =R= : Radiance   –P– : Pleasure

♯ : Falling to the Enemy

Table IX

	region	I	II	III	IV	V	VI	VII	VIII	IX	X	XI	XII
(*a)	PURPLE CREPE MYRTLE	=R=	♯	♯	♯	♯	>T<	♯	♯	–P–	>T<	♯	–P–
(*b)	HEAVEN'S VOID	♯	=R=	♯	♯	♯	♯	>T<	♯	♯	♯	♯	♯
(*c)	HEAVEN'S HONOUR	♯	♯	–P–	♯	>T<	♯	♯	♯	♯	♯	♯	=R=
(*d)	HEAVEN'S SEAL	>T<	♯	♯	=R=	=R=	♯	♯	♯	♯	♯	♯	–P–
(*e)	HEAVEN'S LONGEVITY	♯	♯	–P–	♯	♯	♯	♯	♯	♯	=R=	♯	>T<
(*f)	HEAVEN'S SPACE	♯	♯	♯	♯	♯	♯	♯	♯	♯	♯	♯	♯
(*g)	RED PHOENIX	♯	>T<	–P–	♯	–P–	♯	♯	♯	♯	♯	♯	>T<
(*h)	HEAVEN'S GRANARY	♯	♯	♯	–P–	♯	=R=	>T<	–P–	♯	♯	♯	=R=
(*i)	HEAVEN'S MONEY	♯	♯	♯	>T<	–P–	=R=	–P–	>T<	♯	♯	♯	=R=
(*j)	LITERARY EXCELLENCE	♯	♯	>T<	♯	♯	♯	=R=	♯	♯	♯	>T<	♯
(*k)	HEAVEN'S FORTUNE	♯	♯	=R=	>T<	♯	–P–	♯	♯	♯	♯	♯	♯
(*l)	HEAVEN'S REWARD	♯	♯	♯	–P–	♯	=R=	♯	♯	>T<	♯	♯	♯
(*m)	Heaven's Staff	=R=	♯	♯	♯	♯	♯	♯	=R=	=R=	♯	♯	=R=
(*n)	Heaven's Curiosity	♯	>T<	♯	♯	–P–	♯	♯	>T<	♯	♯	♯	♯
(*o)	Hair and Fur	=R=	♯	>T<	=R=	♯	♯	♯	–P–	♯	♯	–P–	♯
(*p)	Heaven's Axe	♯	♯	–P–	♯	♯	>T<	=R=	♯	>T<	=R=	♯	♯
(*q)	Heaven's Punishment	♯	♯	>T<	♯	♯	♯	–P–	♯	♯	=R=	>T<	♯
(*r)	Heaven's Elegance	♯	♯	♯	>T<	=R=	♯	♯	♯	♯	♯	>T<	–P–
(*s)	Heaven's Lamenting	♯	>T<	♯	=R=	=R=	♯	♯	♯	>T<	♯	♯	♯

Notes

1. The Nine Fortunate Stars in the Temple, Radiance and Pleasure rule over Glory and Honour. If they are absent from these houses then the honours are only slight.
2. If the Nine Unfortunate Stars are in the Temple, Radiance and Pleasure they still indicate good fortune; it is only when they are absent from the Temple, Radiance and Pleasure that they indicate ill fortune.
3. The Heaven's Space Star is not actually a star, but a 'space' where there is no star. Consequently, it is never classed as Temple, Radiance or Pleasure.
4. According to the ancient writers, the stars in the Temple, Radiance and Pleasure never pertain to yang regions, only to yin regions.

Establishing the Twelve Houses of Destiny

As in Western astrology, Chinese horoscopes are divided into twelve 'houses', or divisions which represent various aspects of one's fate or personality. There is considerable variation in the names of the twelve divisions, even in fact in the way in which the twelve divisions are established.

The following is the method which is described in the *Tao Tsang*, and derives from about the sixth century at the latest.

The text informs us that there are twelve 'palaces' of Fate, the principle palace being the 'Fate' palace itself. (The Chinese text uses the term 'palace' for distinctly different meanings, which I have translated by 'region' or 'house' according to the sense.) The position of the House of Fate is determined by the time of birth, and the location of the T'ien Chang [*m] Heaven's Staff Star. Allocate the branch of the birth hour to the region occupied by the [*m] Heaven's Staff, then count out round the face of the horoscope chart mentally until you reach IV (Mao). Obviously if the branch is greater than IV, you must carry on past XII, through I, II and III up to IV. The region where you eventually arrive is the Fate Palace.

Example: if the Heaven's Staff is in Region V (Chen), and the birth hour branch is yin, start at V (Chen), and count III – IV (Yin – Mao); this is two places, so one moves two places from V (Chen) which leads to VI (Ssu).

Table X: The Fate Palaces

Heaven's Staff is in	I	II	III	IV	V	VI	VII	VIII	IX	X	XI	XII
Birth Hour Branch												
I		IV	V	VI	VII	VIII	IX	X	XI	XII	I	II	III
II		III	IV	V	VI	VII	VIII	IX	X	XI	XII	I	II
III		II	III	IV	V	VI	VII	VIII	IX	X	XI	XII	I
IV		I	II	III	IV	V	VI	VII	VIII	IX	X	XI	XII
V		XII	I	II	III	IV	V	VI	VII	VIII	IX	X	XI
VI		XI	XII	I	II	III	IV	V	VI	VII	VIII	IX	X
VII		X	XI	XII	I	II	III	IV	V	VI	VII	VIII	IX
VIII		IX	X	XI	XII	I	II	III	IV	V	VI	VII	VIII
IX		VIII	IX	X	XI	XII	I	II	III	IV	V	VI	VII
X		VII	VIII	IX	X	XI	XII	I	II	III	IV	V	VI
XI		VI	VII	VIII	IX	X	XI	XII	I	II	III	IV	V
XII		V	VI	VII	VIII	IX	X	XI	XII	I	II	III	IV

The Twelve Palaces: Introductory Remarks

1. The Fate and Body Palaces

Once the House of Fate is established, the other eleven houses follow in anticlockwise order. The names of the houses, and the aspects of one's destiny which they rule, are given in the first of the following tables. As a check on the position of the twelve houses, Table XI shows at a glance the location of the twelve houses for any position of the Fate.

I   The Fate
II   Riches and wealth: riches and wealth
III Brothers and kindred: emotions and affections

IV   Land and Dwelling: possessions and inheritance
V   Sons and daughters: kindness, virtue and charitable works
VI   Servants and slaves: one's place in society
VII   Wife and concubines: marriage
VIII   Sickness and distress: health and constitution
IX   Removal and change: foreign travel
X   Official and reward: honours and fame; career
XI   Good fortune and virtue: opportunities in life
XII   Manner and bearing: manner and bearing

Table XI: The Position of the Houses depending on the Region of the Fate

Fate is in		I	II	III	IV	V	VI	VII	VIII	IX	X	XI	XII
		Position of the other houses											
II	Riches and Wealth	XII	I	II	III	IV	V	VI	VII	VIII	IX	X	XI
III	Brothers and Kindred	XI	XII	I	II	III	IV	V	VI	VII	VIII	IX	X
IV	Land and Dwelling	X	XI	XII	I	II	III	IV	V	VI	VII	VIII	IX
V	Sons and Daughters	IX	X	XI	XII	I	II	III	IV	V	VI	VII	VIII
VI	Servants and Slaves	VIII	IX	X	XI	XII	I	II	III	IV	V	VI	VII
VII	Wife and Concubines	VII	VIII	IX	X	XI	XII	I	II	III	IV	V	VI
VIII	Sickness and Distress	VI	VII	VIII	IX	X	XI	XII	I	II	III	IV	V
IX	Removal and Change	V	VI	VII	VIII	IX	X	XI	XII	I	II	III	IV
X	Official and Reward	IV	V	VI	VII	VIII	IX	X	XI	XII	I	II	III
XI	Good Fortune and Virtue	III	IV	V	VI	VII	VIII	IX	X	XI	XII	I	II
XII	Manner and Bearing	II	III	IV	V	VI	VII	VIII	IX	X	XI	XII	I

Method for Establishing the Position of the Body Palace

The Body Palace (there is no Western equivalent) is regarded as determining the length of life, and health. Although several specialist Chinese books on astrology expand on the significance of the Body Palace, it is sufficient here to give the basic principles. Note the peculiarities regarding the division of the days, which I believe derives from the fact that the months are irregular in length. The *Tao Tsang* gives the following procedure for calculating the positions of the stars in their houses:

> The Position of the Body Palace is found by counting from the [region occupied by the] Heaven's Staff [*m] according to the date of the lunar month, reckoning 2½ lunar days per region.
>
> There is no distinction between male and female in the direction of counting. [*This rule would have a greater significance for Chinese astrologers, who would be familiar with fortune-telling methods in which horoscopes for a woman are counted in the reverse direction to those for a man.*]
>
> Regarding the 3rd, 13th, 23rd, 8th, 18th and 28th days of the lunar month [*those in which the odd half-days occur*], these six days at the Wu hour [noon *the seventh branch*] do not cross over to the next region; the cross-over occurs at the Wei [eighth] double-hour [*even though the Wu hour is the seventh double-hour*].

41

Table XII: The Position of the Body Palace

[*m], Tien Chang, Heaven's Staff is in position	I	II	III	IV	V	VI	VII	VIII	IX	X	XI	XII
Day of the Lunar month of birth												
a.m. Day 1 to noon hour Day 3	XII	I	II	III	IV	V	VI	VII	VIII	IX	X	XI
p.m. Day 3 to midnight Day 5	XI	XII	I	II	III	IV	V	VI	VII	VIII	IX	X
a.m. Day 6 to noon hour Day 8	X	XI	XII	I	II	III	IV	V	VI	VII	VIII	IX
p.m. Day 8 to midnight Day 10	IX	X	XI	XII	I	II	III	IV	V	VI	VII	VIII
a.m. Day 11 to noon hour Day 13	VIII	IX	X	XI	XII	I	II	III	IV	V	VI	VII
p.m. Day 13 to midnight Day 16	VII	VIII	IX	X	XI	XII	I	II	III	IV	V	VI
a.m. Day 17 to noon hour Day 18	VI	VII	VIII	IX	X	XI	XII	I	II	III	IV	V
p.m. Day 18 to midnight Day 20	V	VI	VII	VIII	IX	X	XI	XII	I	II	III	IV
a.m. Day 21 to noon hour Day 23	IV	V	VI	VII	VIII	IX	X	XI	XII	I	II	III
p.m. Day 23 to midnight Day 25	III	IV	V	VI	VII	VIII	IX	X	XI	XII	I	II
a.m. Day 26 to noon hour Day 28	II	III	IV	V	VI	VII	VIII	IX	X	XI	XII	I
p.m. Day 28 to midnight Day 30	I	II	III	IV	V	VI	VII	VIII	IX	X	XI	XII

Example: for a person whose Heaven's Staff is in Branch V (Chen) on the 18th day of the Chinese lunar month, the Body Palace is six regions inclusive after V, i.e. in Branch X (Yü).

Remarks concerning the Fate and Body Palaces

Chinese texts maintain that the Fate and Body Palaces should be in agreement. According to the ancient sages, 'The Fate [Palace] gives the actual Body; the Body [Palace] gives its employment.'

If the aspect of both the Fate Palace and the Body Palace is good, it is said that 'the Body's employment is in perfect order.' This kind of Fate reveals complete good fortune.

Conversely, if both the Fate Palace and Body Palace are badly aspected, it is said that 'The Body's employment is not in order.' Put bluntly, it means that this is an indication of ill fortune.

If the Fate is good, but the Body is bad, this is termed 'Possessing Body without employment.' This kind of Fate is said to be 'Early arriving and early departing.'

If the Fate is bad, but the Body is good, this is called 'Possessing Employment, but lacking Body.' This kind of Fate is said to be 'Late in arrival and late in departure.'

The Fate Palace

The following stars are regarded as being in sympathy with the stars of the Fate Palace; the regions which they occupy are known by special terms, which will be referred to shortly.

The Originating Palaces:
    [*k] T'ien Fu, Heaven's Fortune
    [*q] T'ien Hsing, Heaven's Punishment
    [*s] T'ien K'u, Heaven's Lamenting
The Agreement:
    [*e] T'ien Shou, Heaven's Longevity

The Third Harmonic:
    [*g] Hung Luan, The Red Phoenix
    [*r] T'ien Yang, Heaven's Elegance
    [*c] T'ien Kuei, Heaven's Honour
    [*p] T'ien Jen, Heaven's Axe

The Body Palace

Similarly, the Body Palace has its own concordant stars.

The Originating Palaces:
    [*g] Hung Luan, The Red Phoenix
    [*r] T'ien Yang, Heaven's Elegance
The Agreement:
    [*a] Tzu Wei, The Purple Crepe Myrtle
    [*n] T'ien I, Heaven's Curiosity
The Third Harmonic:
    [*k] T'ien Fu, Heaven's Fortune
    [*q] T'ien Hsing, Heaven's Punishment
    [*s] T'ien K'u, Heaven's Lamenting
    [*c] T'ien Kuei, Heaven's Honour
    [*p] T'ien Jen, Heaven's Axe

Understanding the Fate

Now that the regions of the Fate and other houses have been established, the next step is to interpret the significance of the charts. Although this involves the understanding of more esoteric terminology, the principles are very clear.

1. The Root Direction
The house pertaining to the matter under consideration is called the Root Direction.
   Suppose, for example, that the query concerns health or life expectancy. This is the business of the Fate Palace ('The Fate Palace gives the actual body'). Thus, the House of Fate would be the Root Direction.
   Again suppose the question is regarding one's children; then the Root Direction would be the House of Sons and Daughters.

2. The Reflexive Direction
The region directly opposite the Root Direction is called the Reflexive Direction.
   For example, if the Root Direction is Region I, then it is obvious from the 'spider's web' horoscope chart that the Reflexive Direction must be Region VII, and vice versa
   The six pairings are therefore:

I-VII, IV-X: III-XI, VI-XII, II-VIII, V-XI

3. The Harmonious Directions

Palaces three palaces away from the Root Direction are said to be harmonious. Imagine the Root Direction to be at twelve o'clock on a clockface; then the harmonious directions would be at four o'clock and eight o'clock.

The harmonious directions therefore fall into four groups of three, comprising:

XI-I-V, III-VII-XI, VI-X-II, XII-IV-VIII

4. Concordances

The stars which appear in the Root Direction Palace are called concordant; those stars which appear in the Reflexive Palace are said to be discordant; and those which are in palaces harmonious to the Root Direction are said to be harmonious.

Interpreting the Fate

To understand the nature of the Fate Palace, the first step is to compare the Fate Palace with the Root Direction Palace, and see whether the stars in those two palaces are concordant, harmonious or discordant. In general, this will reveal whether the outcome is fortunate or not.

Similarly, examine the Body Palace, again noting the concordant and dissonant stars. Following the precept that 'the Fate gives the Body, and the Body its Employment' one will be able to see whether events in life will be fortunate. What this means is that the Fate gives the general picture with regards to health and life expectation, but the Body Palace tells us what the external forces in life will be like. Another way of summarizing this is to say that the Fate Palace is subjective, the Body Palace objective. It is possible to be healthy and sound in body, but have a useless, wasted life. Conversely, one might be beset with ill health, or disabled, and yet be able to lead a very full and happy life.

The Strong and Weak Houses

Certain 'houses' (seven altogether) are regarded as carrying greater significance than others. The Principle Strong Houses are:

1	The Fate
4	Land and Dwelling
6	Servants and Slaves
10	Official and Reward.

The Secondary Strong Houses are:

5	Sons and Daughters
11	Good Fortune and Virtue.

The Third Rank Strong House:

2	Riches and Wealth

This leaves five 'Weak' houses which are similarly ranked in order of significance.

The Principal Weak Houses are:
12   Manner and Bearing
7   Wife and Concubines

The Secondary Weak Houses are:
8   Sickness and Distress
9   Removal and Change

The Third Rank Weak House is:
3   Brothers and Kindred

The Interpretation of the Fate Palace

Review of Procedure:
So far, we have seen the horoscope chart divided into twelve fixed regions, and the nineteen stars allocated to their respective regions. From the branch of the birth hour, and the location of the star Heaven's Staff [*m] the location of the Fate Palace was fixed, and from that, the respective positions of the other eleven houses of destiny. Finally, from the date of the Chinese month (which is actually the age of the Moon), and the location of Heaven's Staff [*m], it is possible to calculate the position of the Body Palace.

Now that the details of the horoscope have been established, the next step is to interpret the destiny revealed by the positions of the stars in the houses.

Not surprisingly, the first consideration is given to the Fate Palace.

Begin by observing the position of the Fate Palace, and note whether the Fate occurs in its most suited region of the horoscope chart, that is to say, the regions which are known as the Temple, Radiance or Pleasure. (You will probably wish to refer back to Table IX.)

Next, note if there are any auxiliary stars present in the same region (auxiliary stars are those from [*m] to [*s]).

Having established the positions of the Fate stars, consult the list of interpretations given in the following sections to determine whether the Fate can be regarded as auspicious or otherwise.

The Fate Palace

Once the Fate Palace of the horoscope has been established, take note of the principal star in that region, then turn to the relevant paragraph in the following section.

If the principal star in the Fate Palace is: [*a] Tzu Wei, the Purple Crepe Myrtle

Note: For brevity, from this point on the Purple Crepe Myrtle Star [*a] will simply be called 'the Purple Star'.

The Purple Star has its Temple in Regions VI and X. Its Radiance occurs in Region I, and the Pleasure in Regions IX and XII.

The Purple Star also has the names 'Purple Aura', 'The Great Yang', 'The Jade Hall', and 'Minute and Invisible'.

When it is present in the Fate Palace, it shows abundance of honours.

The Residence of Stars which this star rules is the Central Palace of the Heavens. (This is a reference to the region of the sky nearest the Pole Star.)

If the Purple Star is located in the regions I, VI, IX, X, XII, then it must either be in the Temple, the Radiance or the Pleasure. Consequently, it indicates that honours are great, and life will be long. The bearer will wear clothes of rich (imperial) purple and the loins will be girded with gold. Riches are in abundance. Fortune and happiness are assured; life is certain to be long, and not only will the person be learned and refined, but furthermore of handsome countenance.

Sons will enter school and college. Provided that the star [*o] Mao T'ou, Hair and Fur, is not present in the same region, then in youth the son will be prosperous also.

The daughter will be skilful at weaving, sewing and embroidery. Provided that star [*p] T'ien Jen, Heaven's Axe, is not present in the same region, she will bring honour to the house and her name will be revered.

But if the Purple Star has not entered the Temple, the Radiance or the Pleasure, and furthermore if there are unlucky stars present in addition in the same palace, then this is called the Orphan Star. It would be best to become a monk or a nun, and to devote one's life to studying the Tao.

In short, when the Purple Star rules, people and events are fortunate, there is abundance and profit, and everything fattens and prospers.

It indicates that the physique is slim, the trunk slender, and the back broad.

The aura is a deep purple, red, yellow and white. The aura of the youngest son is clear, and pale yellow in colour.

Interpreting the Presence of the Stars in the Various Regions

The general rules for interpreting the stars in the various regions have already been stated, but it would be useful to summarize them again.

The auspices of the stars can be read with some precision if the following principles are kept in mind:

1. The nature of the house determines the general scope of the influence of the stars in that region.
2. The name of the star is a clue to the way in which its influence is manifested. For example, if star [*r] 'Heaven's Elegance' is in a fortunate position, then it could indicate a refined taste and a love of the fine arts; but as an 'unfortunate' star, it would reveal a love of luxury leading to profligacy and waste.
3. If the star is in its Temple, Radiance or Pleasure, then the interpretation can be assumed to be good.
4. If the star is a 'fortunate' star, then its influence can be regarded as good.
5. Even if the star is an 'unfortunate' one, its malign influence can still be counterbalanced if it is in its own Temple, Radiance or Pleasure.

The reader is advised to study the following interpretations of the conjunction of each auxiliary star with star [*b] Heaven's Void in the House of Fate, and relate the interpretations to the five principles outlined above.

If the Principal Star of the Fate Palace is: [*b] T'ien Hsü, Heaven's Void:

The Void Star has its Temple in Region VII, and its Radiance in Region II. It is given the name 'Insubstantial', and it signifies ruin and waste. All those that dwell under its influence grieve much and are hapless. Ambitions remain as dreams. Deeds are never brought to completion.

Yet if the Void Star is in its Temple or Radiance, in regions VII or II, then this reveals glory and splendour, and with the promise of abundant honours. However, in regions III, VI, IX or XII wealth will be of very little substance.

If [*m] Heaven's Staff is present, this means the sentence of death for a crime. Such a person will be avaricious, a drunkard and an addict, and will die young.

If [*n] Heaven's Curiosity is present, this indicates a schemer fond of plotting.

If [*o] Hair and Fur is present, this indicates the loss of wealth.

If [*p] Heaven's Axe is present, the interpretation is the same as for [*m].

If [*q] Heaven's Punishment is present, this indicates a very violent death.

If [*r] Heaven's Elegance is present, this shows lewd behaviour and living out of marriage.

If [*s] Heaven's Lamenting is present, the person will be orphaned.

Heaven's Void indicates extreme misfortune if it occurs in the Riches and Wealth Palace or the Official and Honour Palace.

Interpreting the Twelve Houses of Fate

The foregoing section on the interpretations of the aspects of the fixed stars has dealt exclusively, so far, with the Fate Palace. We have looked at one star in particular, [*a] Tzu Wei the Purple Star, and have looked at each aspect of this star in conjunction with other stars in various regions. Then we examined the significance of each star in the Fate Palace.

Obviously, it would be outside the confines of a single volume to outline the significance of each aspect of the twelve principal stars with the auxiliary stars house by house and region by region. The five general principles, stated earlier, are a proper guide to the understanding of the portents of the fixed stars. But in order to give the reader an insight into the reading of a Chinese horoscope, here are a few of the original comments from an ancient source. By studying these interpretations, and comparing them with the five principles, the reader will achieve a fuller understanding of the working methods used.

I emphasize that the following comments form only a representative collection of observations on the aspects, the purpose behind this selection being principally to help readers to develop skills in making their own objective (or even subjective) comments.

Most people would like to know if they are destined for riches, so it would seem to be pertinent to begin with the 'House of Riches and Wealth', i.e. the second house.

Auspices shown by Each Star in the House of Riches and Wealth

[*a] Tzu Wei, The Purple Star: wealth and fortune.

[*b] T'ien Hsü, Heaven's Void: wealth increases, but its continuation is uncertain.

[*c] T'ien Kuei, Heaven's Honour: riches and a title.

[*d] T'ien Yin, Heaven's Seal: finances will be adequate.

[*e] T'ien Shou, Heaven's Longevity: riches and honours.

[*f] T'ien K'ung, Heaven's Space: riches come and go. It will not be possible to save.

[*g] Hung Luan, The Red Phoenix: average satisfaction.

[*h] T'ien K'u, Heaven's Granary: wealth and prosperity. It is the direct opposite to the 'Destroyer' Star. It indicates a rich marriage; money will not rest idle, but be put to good use.

[*i] T'ien Kuan, Heaven's Money: money will have to be hard-earned; but finances will be balanced, expenditure equalling revenues.

[*j] Wen Ch'ang, Literary Excellence: the whole family will enjoy the benefits of wealth.

[*k] T'ien Fu, Heaven's Fortune: wealth is ample enough.

[*l] T'ien Lu, Heaven's Reward: certain riches.

[*m] T'ien Chang, Heaven's Staff: the middle road is beset with dangers and hazards.

[*n] T'ien I, Heaven's Curiosity: there will be no riches.

[*o] Mao T'ou, Hair and Fur: emptiness, waste, robbery and loss.

[*p] T'ien Jen, Heaven's Axe: modest wealth.

[*q] T'ien Hsing, Heaven's Punishment: after public glory there will be private gain, but greed will lead to ruin.

[*r] T'ien Yang, Heaven's Elegance: a life wasted by flowery living, with money squandered on gambling. The family will be destroyed and punishments will lay waste to possessions and honours will be withdrawn.

[*s] T'ien K'u, Heaven's Lamenting: destruction and waste of wealth and property.

Auspices shown by Each Star in the House of Brothers and Kindred

Note: in the following section, references to 'family' usually refer to 'brothers and sisters' rather than sons or parents.

[*a] Tzu Wei, the Purple Star: there will be many dependants.

[*b] T'ien Hsü, Heaven's Void: dishonour in the family.

[*c] T'ien Kuei, Heaven's Honour: expansion of the family business; great wealth will accrue.

[*d] T'ien Yin, Heaven's Seal: a member of the family will become famous.

[*e] T'ien Shou, Heaven's Longevity: all the family will enjoy long life.

[*f] T'ien K'ung, Heaven's Space: family strife.

[*g] Hung Luan, The Red Phoenix: the family will be closely attached to each other.

[*h] T'ien K'u, Heaven's Granary: strong family ties.

[*i] T'ien Kuan, Heaven's Money: the family will disperse, and family businesses come to an end.

[*j] Wen Ch'ang, Literary Excellence: a close approach to an honourable position, if not to oneself, then to a relative.

[*k] T'ien Fu, Heaven's Fortune: the family will be warm and loving.

[*l] T'ien Lu, Heaven's Reward: all the family will be renowned.

[*m] T'ien Chang, Heaven's Staff: the family will cling to each other like vines.

[*n] T'ien I, Heaven's Curiosity: one brother will have unusual sexual inclinations; the family will not sit at the same table to eat.

[*o] Mao T'ou, Hair and Fur: the family will not get on together.

[*p] T'ien Jen, Heaven's Axe: premature death.

[*q] T'ien Hsing, Heaven's Punishment: the family name will be wiped out.

[*r] T'ien Yang, Heaven's Elegance: the family will be rebellious and unconventional.

[*s] T'ien K'u, Heaven's Lamenting: the family will war against each other.

Auspices shown by Each Star in the House of Land and Dwelling

[*a] Tzu Wei, The Purple Crepe Myrtle: riches and possessions will accrue.

[*b] T'ien Hsü, Heaven's Emptiness: at first there will be possessions, but later, nothing.

[*c] T'ien Kuei, Heaven's Honour: there will be wealth and land to a satisfactory degree.

[*d] T'ien Yin, Heaven's Seal: land and possessions will be acquired.

[*e] T'ien Shou, Heaven's Longevity: land and possessions will be acquired; later in life there will be more gains.

[*f] T'ien K'ung, Heaven's Space: what is possessed will have been hard-earned.

[*g] Hung Luan, The Red Phoenix: estate and property are found in the 'Radiance'.

[*h] T'ien K'u, Heaven's Granary: land and possessions will be acquired.

[*i] T'ien Kuan, Heaven's Money: riches and honours will be received.

[*j] Wen Ch'ang, Literary Excellence: a comfortable cottage with a small but lucrative farm.

[*k] T'ien Fu, Heaven's Fortune: land and possessions will be acquired.

[*l] T'ien Lu, Heaven's Reward: a comfortable cottage with a small but lucrative farm.

[*m] T'ien Chang, Heaven's Staff: there will be losses, in other respects successes.

[*n] T'ien I, Heaven's Curiosity: parents will soon decline. This furthermore indicates a self-made person, rather than one affected by fate.

*Note 1: If [*n] T'ien I, Heaven's Curiosity, occurs alongside [*h], T'ien K'u, The Granary Star, then this indicates at first there will be destruction, but later the family will be rebuilt.*

*Note 2: If [*h] the Granary Star or [*i] T'ien Kuan, Heaven's Money occur alongside [*n] T'ien I, Heaven's Curiosity in the House of Land and Dwelling, this indicates there is great loss at first, but it will be followed by regains and rebuilding.*

[*o] Mao T'ou, Hair and Fur: great loss, followed by great expansion.

[*p] T'ien Jen, Heaven's Axe: losses in some respects, gains in others.

[*q] T'ien Hsing, Heaven's Punishment: as one sows, so one reaps.

[*r] T'ien Yang, Heaven's Elegance: destruction of property.

[*s] T'ien K'u, Heaven's Lamenting: destruction of property.

Auspices shown by Each Star in the House of Sons and Daughters

[*a] Tzu Wei, The Purple Crepe Myrtle: two children, the elder a daughter, the younger a son. The son will be father to a fine grandson.

[*b] T'ien Hsü, Heaven's Void: old age will be childless. There will be a son, full of airs and graces, and dissipated. Evil will befall him in youth. Good and evil fortune reside in the house of the son.

[*c] T'ien Kuei, Heaven's Honour: three children; one son will be fine and strong.

[*d] T'ien Yin, Heaven's Seal: children will establish families of their own. There will be two sons.

[*e] T'ien Shou, Heaven's Longevity: children will establish families of their own. Two sons.

[*f] T'ien K'ung, Heaven's Space: a daughter at first, a son later. The younger son will have a difficult childhood.

[*g] Hung Luan, The Red Phoenix: sons are unlikely but there will be many daughters.

[*h] T'ien K'u, Heaven's Granary: children will establish their own families; there will be two sons.

[*i] T'ien Kuan, Heaven's Money: sadness for a long time, then two sons.

[*j] Wen Ch'ang, Literary Excellence: three fine sons; five children altogether. One child will have exceptionally acute hearing.

[*k] T'ien Fu, Heaven's Fortune: three fine sons; five children altogether. One child will bring rich rewards.

[*l] T'ien Lu, Heaven's Reward: glories and honours will be heaped on the children. Two sons.

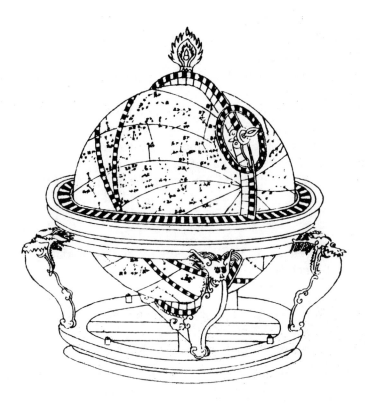

Worksheet 2

Objectives

1. To establish the positions of the Fixed Stars.
2. To establish the positions of the Fate and Associated Houses.

Procedure

1. From Worksheet 1 note the Hour Branch, Year Branch, Day of the Chinese Month, and Chinese Lunar Month.
2. Note the positions of the twelve principal stars, and enter these on the horoscope chart, inner ring.
3. Note the positions of the auxiliary stars, and note these on the horoscope chart, second ring.
4. Note the auspices, Temple, Radiance and Pleasure of the stars.
   Find the positionof the Fate Palace.
5. Note the position of the Twelve Houses on the outer ring of the horoscope chart.

Method

STEP 1. From Worksheet 1, STEP 26, note the following data:
Hour Branch [**HB**]≫
Year Branch [**YB**]≫

STEP 2. From Worksheet 1, STEP 20, note the following data.
Chinese Day of Month [**CD**]≫
The number of the Chinese Lunar Month [**LM**]≫

STEP 3. Use the Year Branch [YB] to find the Region occupied by the Purple Star [*a] as follows:

[YB] →	I	II	III	IV	V	VI	VII	VIII	IX	X	XI	XII
	VIII	IX	X	XI	XII	I	II	III	IV	V	VI	VII → Purple Star Region

Enter the Purple Star [*a] into its appropriate region in the Inner Ring on Horoscope Workchart II.

STEP 4. Assign the eleven remaining principal stars [*b] to [*l] round the Inner Ring of Horoscope Workchart II.

STEP 5. Use the number of the Chinese Lunar Month of birth [LM] to find the region occupied by Heaven's Staff [*m] as follows:

[LM] →	1	2	3	4	5	6	7	8	9	10	11	12
	I	XII	XI	X	IX	VIII	VII	VI	V	IV	III	II → Heaven's Staff

Enter the Heaven's Staff [*m] into its appropriate regions in the Second Ring of Horoscope Workchart I.

STEP 6. Assign the auxiliary stars Heaven's Curiosity [*n], Hair and Fur [*o] and Heaven's Axe [*p] to the Second Ring of Horoscope Workchart I, in the three regions following Heaven's Staff [*m] in anticlockwise order.

STEP 7. Use the number of the Chinese Lunar Month of birth [LM] to find the region occupied by Heaven's Punishment [*q] as follows:

[LM] →	1	2	3	4	5	6	7	8	9	10	11	12	
	X	XI	XII	I	II	III	IV	V	VI	VII	VIII	IX	→ Heaven's Punishment

Enter the Heaven's Punishment [*q] into its appropriate region in the Second Ring of Horoscope Workchart I.

STEP 8. Use the number of the Chinese Lunar Month of birth [LM] to find the region occupied by Heaven's Elegance [*r] as follows:

[LM] →	1	2	3	4	5	6	7	8	9	10	11	12	
	XII	I	II	III	IV	V	VI	VII	VIII	IX	X	XI	→ Heaven's Elegance

Enter the Heaven's Elegance [*r] into its appropriate region in the Second Ring of Horoscope Workchart I.

STEP 9. Use the Branch of the Year of Birth [YB] to find the region occupied by Heaven's Lamenting [*s] as follows:

[YB] →	I	II	III	IV	V	VI	VII	VIII	IX	X	XI	XII	
	II	I	XII	XI	X	IX	VIII	VII	VI	V	IV	III	→ Heaven's Lamenting

STEP 10. From Table VII, note the Fortunate and Unfortunate stars, and mark these into the Horoscope Workchart I in the appropriate places on the Third Ring.

STEP 11. From Table IX, note the Temple, Radiance and Pleasure of the stars, and enter these into the appropriate regions of the Third Ring in Horoscope Workchart I.

STEP 12. Using the birth hour branch [HB] and the position of the Heaven's Staff [*m], find the position of the Fate Palace from Table X. Enter the Fate Palace into its appropriate region of the Outer (fourth) ring of Horoscope Workchart I.

STEP 13. From Table XI, note the positions of the eleven remaining Houses of Fate, and enter these on to Horoscope Workchart I.

STEP 14. Using the Day of the Chinese Lunar Month [CD], and the region occupied by Heaven's Staff [*m], find, from Table XII, the region of the Body Palace. Mark this on Horoscope Workchart I.

STEP 15. Now analyse the horoscope according to the principles outlined in the section 'Interpreting the Fate' (page 44).

Horoscope Workchart I

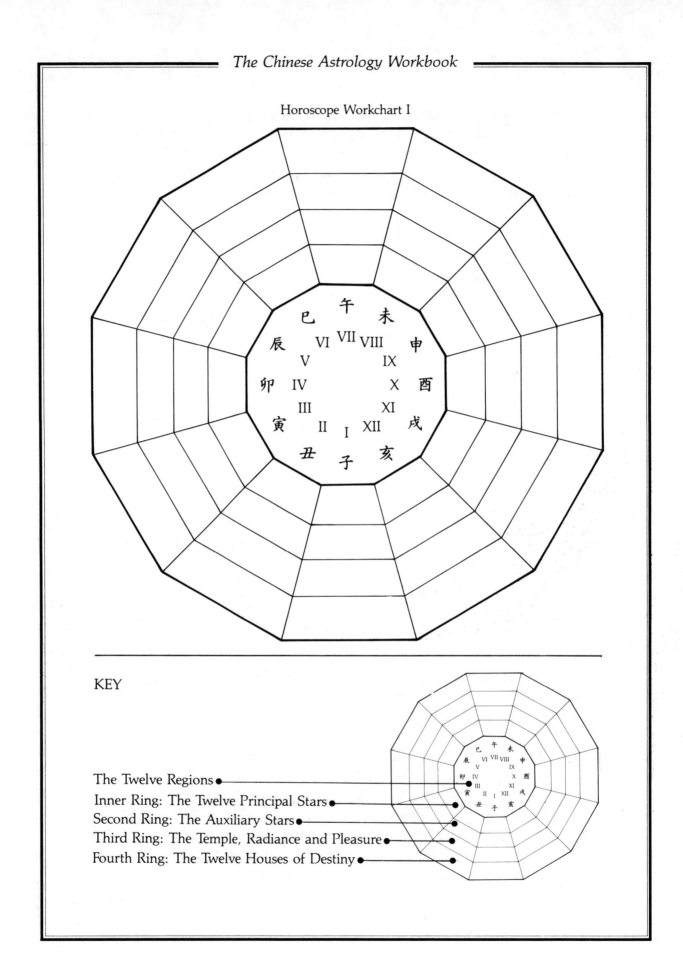

KEY

The Twelve Regions
Inner Ring: The Twelve Principal Stars
Second Ring: The Auxiliary Stars
Third Ring: The Temple, Radiance and Pleasure
Fourth Ring: The Twelve Houses of Destiny

4.

The Twenty-Eight Lunar Mansions

The fundamental difference between Chinese and Western astronomy (and hence, astrology) lies in the way that particular points of the sky are identified. As the sky appears to be in constant motion, some kind of recognizable 'fixed line' has to be decided. There are actually two possibilities, both of which could only have occurred to early astronomers after many years of careful and constant observation. The first thing which the star-watchers would have discovered is that the motions of the skies as a whole are regular: the whole heavenly sphere seems to be in constant rotation about a fixed point, close to what is now called the Pole Star, but which in those far-off days would have been some other star. Of greater interest was the fact that this central point, despite the nightly changing motions of the skies, always lay in a fixed direction. Thus a base-line could be imagined, which would always be a line of reference, no matter what the time of night or season of the year.

Once a reference line such as this had been established, a new discovery would have been made. Although virtually all the stars in the sky seemed to move in unison, the Moon, and five other stars, did not follow the general trend, but pursued their way independently through the sky. (Although we call these 'wandering stars' planets, the Chinese almost invariably, even in astronomical textbooks, use the same word for both 'star' and 'planet'.) Even more interesting was the fact that these six bodies trod roughly the same path through the skies, although at different speeds. Thus, the path which these independent stars followed, which we term the 'ecliptic' could also be used as a base-line.

In the West, the base reference line used by astronomers is the ecliptic; Chinese astronomers, however, have always used the Pole Star as the reference point, and perhaps more than anything, this reveals the greater antiquity of Chinese astronomy.

Once the ancient astronomers had established their reference point, the next stage was to devise some means of referring the rest of the sky to this base-line. They conceived the idea of the Heavenly Sphere, rotating on an axis which led from the observer at the centre, to the Celestial Pole. Because this 'pole' was slanted, it meant that the equator, or 'waist' of this sphere was tilted at an angle to the horizon. This produced another base-line – the Celestial Equator, which Chinese astronomers call the 'Red Path'. The other imaginary line through the sky – the path travelled by the Moon and Planets – is called the 'Yellow Path'. Yellow is the colour associated with the Emperor and the Sun, and the reason for calling the ecliptic the 'Yellow Path' was that it soon became evident to early astronomers that the path followed by the Moon and planets was also the same as that traversed by the Sun. Indeed, the importance of this knowledge lay in the observation that the Full Moon was always directly opposite the Sun in the sky. During the day, the stars are invisible, and at night, there is no Sun – but from the position of the Full Moon it became possible to establish the position of the Sun in the heavens.

But a road without signposts isn't much use. The next stage was to identify stages along this 'Red Path' and the most obvious way of doing this was to identify certain stars which lay along it. Four 'seasonal' stars were chosen to divide the Red Path very roughly into four segments called the Green Dragon, the Red Bird, the White Tiger and the Black Tortoise. In course of time, other stars were used to make the process of identification more precise, and eventually, for some reason which has never been satisfactorily explained, even in the most ancient texts, each quarter was divided into seven, making twenty-eight divisions in all.

Thus the sky was imagined as being divided, like a grapefruit into segments, from the Celestial Pole to the Celestial Equator – but with one peculiarity. The actual divisions are remarkably uneven, ranging from less than one degree to an entire tenth of the heavenly sphere. Each of these twenty-eight divisions is known as a Hsiu, or Lodging House, but more usually translated as 'lunar mansion' because the Moon takes roughly twenty-eight days to complete its circuit of the sky.

As a result, for more than two thousand years Chinese astronomers have always identified the positions of the Sun, Moon and planets by reference to the lunar mansions which they occupy. In other words, the twenty-eight lunar mansions have the same function in Chinese astrology as the zodiac does in Western astrology. However, it would be wrong, for two reasons, to call the twenty-eight mansions a 'zodiac'; firstly, because the name 'zodiac' derives from the fact that most of the constellations in the Western zodiac are names of animals, and secondly, because the term 'zodiac' refers to the path of the Sun, Moon and planets, whereas the twenty-eight lunar mansions are divisions of the sky.

This section on the twenty-eight lunar mansions is primarily concerned with their astrological significance, while the worksheets which follows how you how to calculate the 'notional' and 'actual' lunar mansions for any particular day.

More technical information on the subject of the twenty-eight lunar mansions can be found in the author's *Chinese Astrology*.

The Notional Mansions

One branch of Chinese astrology maintains that the Hsiu (the Chinese term for the 'lunar mansions') rule each day in turn. Chinese almanacs clearly indicate the ruling mansion of the day, since many Chinese people believe that particular tasks will be undertaken more successfully if they are performed on the day which is ruled by the most appropriate mansion. In matters such as weddings and funerals, it is regarded as being of prime importance to select the most judicious day. These elaborate traditions which dictate which days are best suited for work, pleasure, and even certain foods, are often contemptuously dismissed by Westerners as mere superstitious practices, but they are no more curious than the fact that in the Western world, Monday, for example, has long been regarded as the day for doing such mundane chores as washing, Saturday for socializing, and Friday for eating fish.

It is very important to note that the 'lunar' mansions, as listed in the almanac, bear no relation to the positions of the Moon. For this reason I use the term 'notional' when referring to days which bear the names of the mansions, as distinct from the actual mansions themselves.

The Four Palaces

The twenty-eight mansions fall into four 'Palaces' or groups of seven. In each group, the fourth mansion, the middle one of the seven, is the chief mansion, and contains the determining star. Each Palace bears the name of a mega-constellation which fills almost one quarter of the sky, and is associated with a colour, a season, a direction, and one of the Five Elements of Chinese astrology. The associations are logical; the Sun rises in the east, so the east is symbolic of spring, when trees, made of wood, turn green. In winter it is dark (black) and cold, like the north, and rains and floods are frequent.

Autumn is the opposite of spring, so its direction is west; it is the time when metal implements are used for harvesting – or for making war, and the colour of metal is white.

In summer the sun, in the south, is hot, so we have the element Fire, which is red.

Note that the palaces listed here run in reverse order to the course of the seasons. This is because maps of the sky are a mirror image of terrestrial maps. If you face the south, with a star map in your hand, the southern part of the sky will be shown at the bottom of the map, but the eastern sky will be on the left of the map, not the right.

For this reason, the twenty-eight mansions appear on horoscope charts in anticlockwise order.

First, the Four Palaces.

The Dragon Palace
Colour:	Green
Season:	Spring
Direction:	East
Element:	Wood

The Tortoise Palace
Colour:	Black
Season:	Winter
Direction:	North
Element:	Water

The Tiger Palace
Colour:	White
Season:	Autumn
Direction:	West
Element:	Metal

The Bird Palace
Colour:	Red
Season:	Summer
Direction:	South
Element:	Fire

This leaves one of the Chinese elements – Earth – unaccounted for. The reason is that the Earth element, by definition, belongs to the Earth, and does not appear as one of the celestial palaces. We will find more about it in a later section on the Five Elements.

Names of the Twenty-Eight Mansions

Each Palace contains seven mansions. The fourth mansion of each palace, that is the middle one of the seven, is the chief mansion, and contains the determining star of the Palace. As an example, the Bird Star, Alfard, is the star which determines the location of the Bird Palace, of which the central mansion is the Bird.

The Green Dragon of Spring
(1)		The Horn
(2)		The Neck
(3)		The Base
(4)	*	The Room
(5)		The Heart
(6)		The Tail
(7)		The Basket

The Black Tortoise of Winter
(8)		The Ladle
(9)		The Ox-boy
(10)		The Maiden
(11)	*	The Void
(12)		The Rooftop
(13)		The House
(14)		The Wall

The White Tiger of Autumn
(15)		Astride
(16)		The Mound
(17)		The Stomach
(18)	*	The Pleiades
(19)		The Net
(20)		The Beak
(21)		Orion

The Red Bird of Summer
(22)		The Well
(23)		Ghosts
(24)		The Willow
(25)	*	The Bird
(26)		The Bow
(27)		The Wings
(28)		The Carriage

The notional mansion for any particular day can be calculated very simply from tables, and the way to do this is explained on the next worksheet.

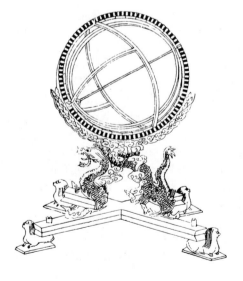

Worksheet 3 – Calculating the Notional Mansion for any day

Objective

To calculate the Notional Mansion for any day.

Procedure

Add the codes for the year and date, with a leap-year adjustment if necessary.
If the total is greater than 28, subtract 28; the result is the number of the Notional Mansion.

Method

STEP 1.   Note the date for which the Notional Mansion is required.
From Table II (page 26-8) Column D, note the Code Number for the day.
[a]≫

STEP 2.   From Table XIII on page 60, note the Code Number for the year.   [b]≫

STEP 3.   If the date in question is 29 February or later in a leap year, add 1, otherwise add 0.   [c]≫

STEP 4.   Add (a) + (b) + (c).   [d]≫

STEP 5.   If (d) is greater than 28, subtract 28 and note the remainder. Otherwise enter (d).   [e]≫

STEP 6.   The figure at (e) is the number of the Notional Mansion.

Check

Notional mansions always occur on the same day of the week. Check your result from the following:

1,	8,	15,	22,		Thursday
2,	9,	16,	23,		Friday
3,	10,	17,	24,		Saturday
4,	11,	18,	25,	*	Sunday
5,	12,	19,	26,		Monday
6,	13,	20,	27,		Tuesday
7,	14,	21,	28,		Wednesday

Table XIII: Year Numbers to find the Notional Mansion

1901	5	1921	2	1941	27	1961	24	1981	21
1902	6	1922	3	1942	0	1962	25	1982	22
1903	7	1923	4	1943	1	1963	26	1983	23
1904	8	1924	5	1944	2	1964	27	1984	24
1905	10	1925	7	1945	4	1965	1	1985	26
1906	11	1926	8	1946	5	1966	2	1986	27
1907	12	1927	9	1947	6	1967	3	1987	0
1908	13	1928	10	1948	7	1968	4	1988	1
1909	15	1929	12	1949	9	1969	6	1989	3
1910	16	1930	13	1950	10	1970	7	1990	4
1911	17	1931	14	1951	11	1971	8	1991	5
1912	18	1932	15	1952	12	1972	9	1992	6
1913	20	1933	17	1953	14	1973	11	1993	8
1914	21	1934	18	1954	15	1974	12	1994	9
1915	22	1935	19	1955	16	1975	13	1995	10
1916	23	1936	20	1956	17	1976	14	1996	11
1917	25	1937	22	1957	19	1977	16	1997	13
1918	26	1938	23	1958	20	1978	17	1998	14
1919	27	1939	24	1959	21	1979	18	1999	15
1920	0	1940	25	1960	22	1980	19	2000	16

The Actual Mansion

The 'notional' mansion has very little to do with astrology proper, because it is not calculated according to the positions of any stellar body. But it is possible to make a rough estimation of the actual residence of the Moon with only the minimum of astronomical knowledge. Country astrologers and wandering monks could scarcely have access to complicated ephemerides, which would not only have been rare and extremely costly, but bulky and cumbersome for the traveller to carry. However, for thousands of years itinerant soothsayers carried on their travels some remarkable 'divining' boards – actually scrolls of painted cloth which could be conveniently rolled up and stowed away in a knapsack – on which various calculations could be carried out with the aid of small stones or shells for counters. We have already seen some evidence of this in the instructions given to find the 'Tzu Wei' stars, where the instructions to count forwards or backwards relate to the use of these 'divining' boards. Now we shall look at a simple way to find the approximate location of the Moon.

It is common knowledge that the Full Moon rises as the Sun sets, because the Full Moon is always opposite the Sun. We can use this fact to forecast the position of the Full Moon. All the other information we need is obtained from the Chinese and Western calendars.

Our own calendar is solar, that is to say, it is regulated to suit the progress of the Sun so that by and large, the solstices always occur on the same dates each year. However, the Chinese calendar is lunar, being regulated by the phases of the Moon. Thus, while on any Western date, we are able to give the Sun's position in the sky with some precision, by the same token, using the Chinese calendar enables us to tell the phase of the Moon – New on the first day of the month, and Full on the fifteenth.

The third useful fact is that the Chinese divide the circle into 365¼ degrees, one degree for every day in the year. This is not so far removed from the 360 degrees of Western mathematics, so for the purpose of these calculations we can say that the Sun travels roughly one degree every day.

What this amounts to is that for any given day, we can find the Sun's position with a fair degree of accuracy.

From the Chinese calendar, we know that on the fifteenth of the Chinese lunar month, the Moon is full, and consequently directly opposite the Sun. Since the position of the Sun is known from a calendar table, the Moon must be in the mansion directly opposite.

For days other than the Full Moon, it is only necessary to count from that point as many degrees as days to or from the next Full Moon.

The Sun's positions throughout the year are given in Table II (page 26), Column E, and a diagram showing the twenty-eight lunar mansions, on which solar and lunar positions can be plotted, is given on page 64.

Worksheet 4 – Estimating the Moon's Position

Objective

To estimate the mansion occupied by the Moon on any day.

Procedure

1. Find the mansion occupied by the Sun on the day in question.
2. Calculate the Chinese date according to Worksheet 1.
3. Find the nearest date which would be the 15th day of the Chinese month.
4. Enter the position of the Sun on the 15th day on the Chart of the Lunar Mansions.
5. Count the number of days to the day in question.
6. Count the same number of degrees from the solar position.
7. Take the point on the chart directly opposite the solar position to give the lunar position of the day in question.

Method

STEP 1.   Enter the date for which the Moon's lunar mansion is required.   **date≫**

STEP 2.   From Table II (page 26), Column A, note the Daily Code Number (amended if necessary to account for dates occurring in a leap year on or after 29 February).   **A [dcn] of date≫**

STEP 3.   From Table III (page 28), Central Block, find the line of figures corresponding to the year of the required date.
    Find the figure which is the nearest one below the Daily Code Number. (NOTE: Ignore the right-hand figure 1 in the split columns for the eleventh and twelfth months.)
    Enter nearest monthly code number: **B≫**

STEP 4.   Add 15 to the nearest monthly code number.
    Enter [B] + 15 =   **C≫**

STEP 5.   Return to Table II. Find the date which corresponds to the figure C. This is the date of the Full Moon closest, or next closest, to the required date.
    Enter date of Full Moon: **Full Moon≫**

STEP 6.   Note the number of days difference between the required date and the date of the Full Moon, and whether the Full Moon is before or after the date in question.
    Enter number of days: **Difference≫**
    Enter 'before' or 'after'   **Before/after≫**

STEP 7.   From Table II, column E, find the number of the Solar Mansion on the day of the Full Moon.
    Enter Solar Mansion: **Solar Mansion≫**

STEP 8.   From Table II, column E, look upwards along column E and count the number of days on which the Sun was in the same solar mansion prior to the date of the Full Moon, to give the Solar Mansion Degrees.
Enter number of days: **Solar Mansion Degrees**≫

Now Turn to Horoscope Workchart II

STEP 9.   On Horoscope Workchart II, find the segment corresponding to the Solar Mansion, calculated above in STEP 7.
Find and mark the point on the scale equal to the Solar Mansion Degrees in STEP 8.

STEP 10.   Place a ruler or straight edge on the chart, and mark the point on the scale directly opposite the Solar Mansion Degrees. This gives the position of the Full Moon.
Find and mark the position of the Full Moon.

STEP 11.   On the central, blank band of Horoscope Workchart II, note the segment corresponding to the position of the Full Moon.

STEP 12.   Refer to STEP 6 and note the Difference, and before/after:
Difference≫   **Before/after**≫

On the central, blank, band of the chart, count out as many divisions as the Difference.
Count anticlockwise for 'before' and clockwise for 'after'.
The corresponding mansion on the outer band is the mansion occupied by the Moon on the day in question.

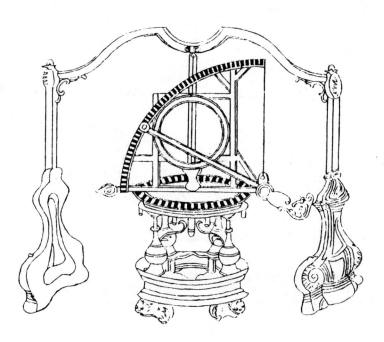

Horoscope Workchart II

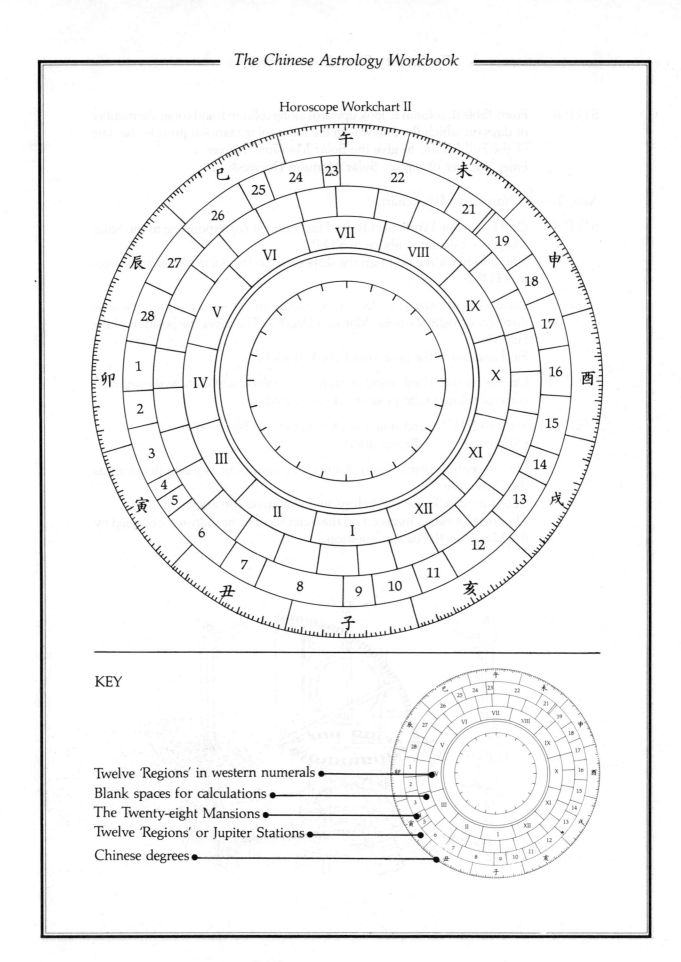

KEY

Twelve 'Regions' in western numerals •
Blank spaces for calculations •
The Twenty-eight Mansions •
Twelve 'Regions' or Jupiter Stations •
Chinese degrees •

The Symbolism of the Twenty-Eight Lunar Mansions

We have met with the *notional* and *actual* lunar mansions. The notional is used to determine what actions are most appropriate for a particular day, while the actual lunar mansion is of more relevance to horoscopic astrology.

Basically, the way that the lunar mansions reveal one's fate can be determined in two ways: firstly from the presence of the Celestial Messengers, that is to say, the planets, and secondly, from the direction in which the mansions lie. To begin with, let us take a look at the symbolism of the twenty-eight mansions themselves.

Mansion 1 – The Horn

The Horn is the Horn of the Dragon, the point from which the twenty-eight mansions are reckoned. Anciently it symbolized the beginning of spring, and is associated with the Spring Equinox. For this reason, it is particularly associated with the second month of the Chinese calendar, which always includes the Spring Equinox.

As the spring is associated with rains, the notional mansion 1 is also thought to forecast mild rain in the spring, and a wet winter.

It is regarded as an extremely fortunate mansion, presiding over growth, creation, birth, horticulture, and agriculture.

Days which are ruled by the Horn are considered to be extremely fortunate for commencing any project; for beginning the construction of a building, or buying land which is going to be used for a long time, or even for embarking on a long-term partnership. Parents therefore like to choose such a day as being especially auspicious for marriages. It is believed that a man who chooses this day to marry will receive promotion, acclaim and great honours. It is ideal for those entering into a political career, as it brings them into contact with the heart of government.

On the other hand, it is not a good day for the finishing of projects, and the winding up of affairs ought to be left to a more appropriate day. Indeed, it would be extremely unlucky to arrange a funeral or memorial service on this day. It is said that a family that does so could expect ill fortune to befall them within three years, either through epidemic, accident or loss of wealth.

Mansion 2 – The Neck

The Neck of the Dragon is the first constellation to be mentioned in the *I Ching*, and there refers to an eclipse of the Sun. It is also associated with the Chinese 'New Year' and consequently is auspicious for celebrations, holidays and gatherings. It presides over illnesses.

It is the ruling mansion for matters to do with the judgement of prisoners, and therefore is concerned with the release of persons who are already in custody. If it is favourable, it shows trust, faithfulness, loyalty, and peace.

Days which are ruled by the Neck are negative. It is not a good day to begin work on any large undertaking, or for construction. A man who accepts promotion on such a day will lose office eventually.

All family gatherings should be avoided; neither weddings nor funerals should be contracted on this day lest one of the guests drop dead while attending.

Certain forecasts regarding the weather are taken from the Neck. If the first day of spring begins with the Neck, it is a sign of violent storms; if the Neck begins the first day of summer, the heat will be oppressive; if the first day of autumn, a wet harvest will follow; if the first day of winter, there will be dry storms. (In these cases, the first day of the season is calculated according to the Chinese calendar of twenty-four terms. See page 95.)

Mansion 3 – The Base

The Base is probably the 'floor' of the 'house' in Mansion 4, the two mansions probably being originally parts of the same constellation. It is concerned with the breaths of spring; when occupied by a fortunate star, it indicates that the rains of spring will be mild, sweet and fruitful. But if it is occupied by a malevolent star, it reveals dampness, mildew, decay and the illnesses which arise from them.

The maladies which are brought about by this constellation are thought to be the chastisement for a failure to pay due respect to one's elders, parents or ancestors. It is therefore a warning to make sure that one's house is in order, that there are no outstanding favours to be repaid, and that one has been straightforward in dealings with other people.

Days which are ruled by the Base are unlucky for the signing of marriage contracts (we would say 'getting engaged'). If this is neglected, evil persons will be attracted to the house – possibly another reference to the following mansion. Furthermore, the children born of a marriage contracted on this day would be poor, and unable to express themselves either through diffidence or handicap.

There are further warnings against travelling by boat on this day, since it is likely to be wrecked – in this case the 'base' represents the ocean floor.

Its meteorological significance is wind and rain in spring, strong winds and rain in summer, storms in autumn, and hurricanes in winter.

Mansion 4 – The Room

When the seven constellations of the Eastern Palace of Spring were all in one constellation, the stars which are now called the Room represented the stomach of the Dragon. This is the chariot of the Sun, and the constellation associated with the Great Sacrifice; it is associated with the Sun, because the Notional Mansion always occurs on a Sunday, but some astrologers maintain that it properly belongs to the planet Jupiter (the Wood Planet) while in ancient times it was held to be the domain of the Fire Planet – Mars. In any event, it is regarded as an extremely fortunate sign.

Not surprisingly, it is concerned with the interiors of houses and buildings, and is fortunate for all matters pertaining to the fabric and interiors of offices, shops and dwellings.

Days which are ruled by the Room are extremely fortunate. Those who erect buildings on a 'Room' day will eventually extend their buildings, increase their holdings and adjoining land, and reap the advantages of a prosperous business.

It was the custom for a wealthy man to take a concubine to raise more sons, and this was accounted a fortunate day to bring a new concubine into the house, as it would ensure him a son within three years. A modern interpretation of this might be to say that this would be a good day for entering into a contract for surrogate parenthood.

Although the usual case is that those days which are fortunate for joyous events were unsuitable for sorrowful ones, the Room is so fortunate a constellation that it is even propitious for funerals and burials to be held on this day, since one's ancestors would be delighted to help in securing promotion, riches, and recognition by those in authority.

Mansion 5 – The Heart

The Heart is, of course, the Heart of the Dragon. It is therefore the symbol of the Emperor, imperial power, supreme authority and wealth. It is not, however, a fortunate constellation, since it bodes conflict with authority, revolution, retribution and punishment. It shows the adverse effects of attempting to be too ambitious, carelessness with one's position, and over-confidence.

Because the mansion is so narrow, and traversed by the celestial bodies very quickly, it signifies speed, quickness of action, and sudden change.

It also indicates the necessity to sell property in order to pay off debts.

Days which are ruled by the Heart are unfortunate for construction – misfortune will result – or for those involved in criminal charges – the verdict is likely to be guilty, and the sentence imprisonment.

Marriages should not be contracted on this day lest the children be afflicted.

Mansion 6 – The Tail

This mansion represents the tail of the Dragon. Just as the Heart represented the Emperor, so the Tail represents the Heir Apparent – the young prince still of an age when he would be kept in the women's apartments. It therefore pertains to young children, mothers, nurses and the weaning of children.

Also, from the symbolism of the heir apparent comes its association with inheritance and legacies. If the mansion is occupied by a fortunate star, it shows wealth through inheritance.

It has been described as 'that which separates Wood from Water'. This can be understood to mean, astrologically, the Wood and Water planets, Jupiter and Mercury, while the literal interpretation is of boats, dams, drains, breakwaters, dykes and the like.

Days which are ruled by the Tail are fortunate for building and for finding hidden treasure, while those whose marriages have been negotiated on a Tail day will have numerous descendants, and be promoted to high office later in life.

Mansion 7 – The Basket

This constellation is thought of as the 'winnowing basket' in Chinese literature. The T'ang Dynasty poet Han Yü complained that he was at the mercy of the Winnowing Basket, which had kept all the wheat, and given him the chaff. Yet the constellation is normally seen as an auspicious one, the Basket being the symbol of plenty.

The concept of the Basket as a winnowing basket, however, seems to be a new one. In ancient times it was regarded as a basket for collecting dung – it was, after all, situated at the Dragon's tail-end. In an agricultural community, manure is highly valued, and it was actually this commodity which gave the mansion its symbolism of riches.

Manure, however, holds little attraction for the city-dweller or literary gentleman, and while the 'winnowing-basket' is more acceptable in polite society, the stigma of the dung-basket resulted in the mansion acquiring a secondary, dubious interpretation – that of gossip, slander and pornography. Thus, when occupied by a fortunate star, the symbolism is of riches and good fortune; when occupied by a malevolent star, it indicates infamy and vices of all kinds.

Days which are ruled by the Basket are ideal for starting new ventures, which will enjoy a year of good fortune. Business will thrive and profits will be handsome. It is a good day to acquire new property, or to open a new door. In present-day terms, this indicates a fortunate day to add extensions to property, to move into new premises, or perhaps to enrol in a new organization which would involve moving into new buildings, as those who do so can be sure of rewards for themselves and their families.

It is also regarded as a fortunate day for burial.

Mansion 8 – The Ladle

In ancient texts, this mansion was known as 'the head of the tortoise' because it is the first mansion in the Black Tortoise Palace of Winter. Its shape somewhat resembles the stars of the Plough (the seven major stars of the Great Bear) which the Chinese called 'the Ladle', although it has only six stars, and for that reason this mansion became commonly known as the Southern Ladle, somewhat confusingly in view of the importance to astrology of the 'Northern Ladle', already encountred in the earlier section on the stars of the Purple Crepe Myrtle.

Because it resembles a measuring can in shape, it signifies filling up, the measuring out of rewards, recompense for good deeds, and rises in salary. It represents satisfaction through completion. It presides over liquids, and is therefore the presiding sign for wine-merchants, and the sellers of liquids. In modern terms of course, this could be extended to include oil and liquid fuel, and represent the oil industry.

Days which are ruled by the Ladle are fortunate for building, digging, and any kind of physical labour. It is an exceedingly fortunate sign, revealing promotion and increase in wealth.

Mansion 9 – The Ox-Boy

A famous legend surrounds this and the next constellation, the Maiden. There was, in the heavens, a beautiful maiden so renowned for her skill in weaving that she wove the garments for the gods. It was her custom to bathe in the river where the Ox-Boy took his charges to water them, and inevitably the two met and fell in love. But they became so infatuated with each other – as young couples in love are apt to do – that they had no thought for anything else; she left her weaving, and he his herds.

The gods were of course very angry at this, and decided that matters could not continue, and parted the two lovers for eternity by the river where they first met. The two can be seen to this day, as the stars Altair, the Ox-Boy, and Vega, the Weaving Maiden, separated for ever by the River Han – or as we know it, the Milky Way. But legend also recounts that once a year, on the feast of the Double Seventh – the seventh day of the seventh Chinese lunar month – magpies gather in the sky to form a bridge on which the lovers can meet.*

Astrologically, the symbolism of this mansion is generally unfortunate, the imagery being derived from the sorrow of the young lovers. Thus, the Ox-Boy signifies barriers, difficulties, and obstacles. It presages ill-fated romances, broken marriages and discord. The Ox-Boy's dissolute behaviour suggests waste, loss of provisions, and carelessness. The wandering oxen signal a warning against leaving doors open, from which is derived insecurity, a failure to take precautions against loss or theft, and insufficient insurance. It indicates sickness and starvation, especially of animals.

On tangible matters, it presides over fields, pathways, roads and the division of land, and if coincident with the House of Land and Dwelling, will emphasize the ground, rather than the buildings which stand on it. In such a case, it depends on what stars are present to establish whether or not the aspects are fortunate.

Days which are ruled by the Ox-Boy are unlucky; the various portents described above are likely to be the lot of those who enter into marrige on an Ox-Boy day, while it is generally unsuitable for contracting any kind of business, as the parties to the contract are deemed likely to lose interest in the project.

Mansion 10 – The Maiden

The legend of the Maiden and the Ox-Boy is given above. Curiously perhaps, considering the Maiden's own unsuccessful romance, the Maiden is the patroness of all girls who wish to marry, and have a rich dowry so as to obtain a handsome husband. It therefore symbolizes marriage, and by extension, the construction of new houses in which young couples might live. The companion sign to the Ox-Boy, when this sign coincides with the House of Land and Dwelling, it emphasizes the building, rather than the ground. Again, in such a case, it is the presence of relevant stars in the House which determines whether this mansion is fortunate.

Otherwise, it is generally an unfortunate sign, revealing disputes and quarrels, and physical violence.

Days which are ruled by the Maiden are unsuitable for funerals, which if carried out on a Maiden day, will result in epidemics and illness, particularly of the bowels, befalling the family; the clear inference is an outbreak of food-poisoning following the funeral meal.

Mansion 11 – The Void

This is the central mansion of the Black Tortoise Palace, and is the pivot of the northern region of winter. It therefore signifies desolation, emptiness, cold, stagnation, hibernation and the tomb.

It presides over cemeteries, tombs, funerals, undertakers, grave-diggers and wills. But as it is the mansion of cold and hibernation, a present-day interpretation would suggest

---

*Not only is this a charming legend, it is also extremely interesting to historians, as it contains specific clues to the antiquity of Chinese astrology. Readers will find more information on pages 110–12 of the author's *Chinese Astrology*.

that it also presides over the frozen food industry.

Days which are ruled by the Void portend domestic quarrels.

It is not a suitable day for digging or construction, while those unwise enough to marry on a Void day can expect to have delinquent children.

Mansion 12 – The Rooftop

The three red stars of this constellation symbolize the Roof of the House in the next mansion. However, the Chinese name of this mansion actually means 'danger', the redness of the stars suggesting that the roof of the house is on fire. Its symbolism, however, has more to do with the 'house' than the rooftop. The mansion presides over fortifications, defences and earthworks, while any kind of building works and construction also come under its aegis.

Days which are ruled by the Rooftop are fraught with danger for those on the move. Travelling should be avoided; those going by land are in danger of being attacked, while ships may run aground or capsize. A much wiser course would be to confine activities to those which can be carried out in one place, such as repairs or refurbishment of houses, especially, of course, to the roof.

Mansion 13 – The House

This mansion has sometimes been called 'The Burning House' on account of its 'burning roof' in the previous mansion. But it is not at all as ominous as it might seem. It is not a house on fire, but a kind of beacon – a tower with a fire burning on top. Judging from the astrological symbolism, the fire must have been a sacred or sacrificial one, burning in a specially constructed building or temple. The House therefore represents a sacrifice to the gods. As a consequence, it is held to be an extremely fortunate sign, the sacred fire being a sign of riches and wealth, while the association with the temple indicates correct conduct and honest dealings.

Days which are ruled by the House are fortunate for construction and building. It is favourable for all projects which are initiated on this day. Those in authority will recognize good work, and give rewards from which the whole family will be able to benefit.

Mansion 14 – The Wall

This is the 'wall' of the 'house' in the previous mansion. Ancient texts suggest that it was the wall of a treasury, or perhaps the temple of the god of wealth. The symbolism is of a store-house of fine treasures – books, paintings and fine art generally. It is therefore associated with virtue, scholarship and the connoisseur.

Nearly always this is a fortunate sign; if, however, it is aspected by an extremely unfavourable star, it takes on the symbolism of a fish's mouth, from which lies issue. Thus, in specific rare cases, the reference to books and literature may indicate libellous or mischievous writing.

Days which are ruled by the Wall are fortunate for expansion, for construction, building and digging. It is a favourable time to embark on new ventures, or enter through new doors. Those who marry today will have extremely talented children.

Mansion 15 – Astride

The constellation shows a man with his legs astride, while some commentators say that the shape of the stars resembles the sole of a shoe. There are several interpretations of this mansion. It symbolizes the Emperor's arsenal and therefore signifies arms, weaponry and preparations for military action. Another source gives it as presiding over canals. As a shoe, it signifies clothing, especially winter clothing such as padded jackets, so warning of the need to prepare for winter, or leaner times ahead. It presides over the garment industry, and textile processes including laundering.

Days which are ruled by Astride are unfavourable for construction work or digging. Riches will not be attracted to any buildings erected on an Astride day, while those who dig trenches on this day will encounter misfortune.

Mansion 16 – The Mound

The 'mound' shows grain piled high. It is the sign of a fine harvest, autumn fairs, and all the rejoicing and festivities which go with them.

Such merry-making reveals this to be the symbol of great assemblies of people, as at conventions and rallies, and also events when large numbers of people are gathered together in harmony. In particular, it presides over people gathered in choirs or orchestras. It shows happy family reunions, concord, and peace between nations.

It is mildly cool and wet, and its meteorological indications are cool winds in spring, mist in summer, fine rain in autumn, and ice in winter. This fortunate sign promises a rich harvest. Days which are ruled by the Mound are favourable for family gatherings, social events, parties, festivities and assemblies of all descriptions.

It is a fortunate day for all kinds of building and construction, digging trenches, and opening watercourses. In particular, it is the ideal day for erecting a triumphal arch, which by extension means unveiling monuments or erecting dedicatory plaques.

Those who marry today will have children destined to become rich.

Mansion 17 – The Stomach

The name 'stomach' is figurative; the constellation represents the granary of the gods, a celestial barn where the harvest was stored. Generally, therefore, it is the sign of the accumulation and storing of great fortune and wealth. It is therefore fortunate for matters concerning investment, savings and banking.

Its inverse meaning, however, taken from the sense of things being locked up, is a prison. When unfavourably aspected, or occupied by a malevolent star, this mansion indicates punishments, imprisonment and execution.

It presides over earthworks, which were built to contain, or store up, water such as the construction of sea-walls, reservoirs and canals.

Days which are ruled by the Stomach are good for putting away savings. It is a fortunate day for any matters involving the Earth element, such as digging, building walls, and even burial of the dead.

Those who are wise enough to choose this day to marry will have children destined to meet the Head of State.

Mansion 18 – The Pleiades

The Chinese name for this mansion – Mao – has no other meaning. The constellation of the Pleiades – to the right of the head of Orion – is a distinctive cluster of small stars, faint on their own, but distinguishable as a group.

Ancient Chinese astronomers, who were more concerned about the appearance and colour of the constellations than the angles made between them and the wandering planets, held that when the Pleiades flickered it signalled an invasion. They were said to be the ears and eyes of Heaven, and so presided over judgments and trials. If they shone clear and bright, an acquittal could be expected, but if they were dull or obscured, it meant a conviction.

Both the symbolism of the invasion, and association with trials and punishments, lead to the Pleiades being regarded as the omen of an untimely death.

Days which are ruled by the Pleiades are regarded as being unlucky. It is not a favourable time to begin construction, digging or any kind of family activity.

Those unfortunate enough to marry on a Pleiades day will soon separate.

Mansion 19 – The Net

The stars forming this constellation include another cluster, the Hyades, which suggest a close-meshed net. Thus this is the symbol of hunting parties, which was carried out partly to rid the land of unwelcome wild beasts, partly for food, and partly for military training.

The accumulation of game for food suggests prosperity and good living. However, continuing the notion of hunting, it also came to signify outlaws, deserters and traitors. It is also called 'The Foreign Carriage' and represents trouble at frontiers.

As the Hyades have been traditionally associated with the rainy season, the Net signifies rain.

Days which are ruled by the Net are generally fortunate, whether for construction work, or burial.

Those who marry on a Net day will have long-lived children.

Mansion 20 – The Beak

This is the smallest mansion of all, only about a degree in width, and traversed by the Moon in a matter of hours. The 'beak' – said to be the beak of a turtle – is composed of the three stars which form the 'head' of Orion and according to one ancient authority is the head of the 'white tiger' of autumn. In this respect, it is worth noting that the 'heads' of the other three Palaces (the Dragon, the Tortoise, and the Bird) occur in mansions 1, 8 and 22, each the first mansion of the respective Palaces.

The Beak presides over those animals which congregate in large numbers, such as cattle and sheep. Since cattle and sheep are guarded by their herdsmen, by extension the Beak presides over people who are under protection – children, especially orphans, the infirm, hostages, prisoners and those in danger.

It is not generally a fortunate sign; many of the portents are concerned with punishment and retribution for wrongdoing, although if the right course of action were always followed, there would be no danger.

On days which are ruled by the Beak, it is important to be extremely careful in one's conduct.

Mansion 21 – Orion

Like Mao, the Pleiades, the Chinese name for this mansion, Shen, originally had no other meaning. The stars of this constellation – which together with the three stars of the preceding constellation are known to us as Orion – are so bright that they outshine the familiar shape of the Great Bear, and on a frosty night in winter make a splendid sight.

Because the top three stars of the constellation were 'removed' to form the mansion of the Beak, Orion signifies decapitation, and consequently, executions, murders, massacres and sudden death. It is also regarded as the guardian of frontiers, over which it presides.

It has both fortunate and unfavourable influences, depending on whether one has been meritorious in one's conduct or not. It is also said to bring merit by directing the favourable influences of the Literary Star.

Days which are ruled by Orion fortunate in some respects, unfortunate in others. Merit will be achieved through building, or beginning new projects. New ventures prosper. Any labour or industry undertaken on an Orion day will be rewarded, whether it is already under way or just commenced.

Conversely, Orion has an adverse influence on attempts to bring any affairs to a close; matters will not end as hoped, but will continue to make demands on time and finance. Marriages and betrothals ought not to be contracted today, lest they end in separation. Nor is it a good day for internments, as this may forebode the death of a distant relative.

Mansion 22 – The Well

Whereas the Beak (Mansion 20) was the narrowest mansion, so the Well is by far the widest. In Western astrological terms, it spans more than a complete sign of the zodiac, equivalent to the stars of Gemini on a star map, although not astrologically. This is the first mansion in the Palace of the Red Bird, and is sometimes known more poetically as the Head of the Phoenix. Not surprisingly, the Well presides over the element Water, and all matters to do with water-courses, canals, reservoirs, and matters to do with water, such as cleansing, water-mills and water transport. From the image of cleansing comes the notion of the cleansing of guilt or debts, and therefore it also presides over honest dealings, law and regularity. Its ruling planet, however, is not Mercury, the Water Planet, but Jupiter, the Wood Planet.

Being such a wide mansion, the Well's influence is largely dissipated, and is regarded as being neither strongly fortunate nor unfortunate.

Days which are ruled by the Well are favourable for most courses of action, although for those taking examinations which come under the aegis of the element Water, the signs are particularly encouraging. Wood, representing plants, and water, suggest that the Well is a beneficial sign for herbivorous animals – cattle, sheep, horses, deer, rabbits – and animal husbandry generally. It also augurs good prospects for widows who own land, which will increase in value, bringing them the security of an income and the chance of a second husband.

It is regarded as an unfortunate time to lay work to one side; that which has been commenced ought to be completed or continued during the influence of the Well, which favours industriousness rather than leisure.

Burials and funerals are not advised on a Well day, as sudden death or epidemic within the family may follow.

Mansion 23 – Ghosts

The name of this very narrow mansion is sometimes translated as 'Imp' or 'Demon' but there should be no doubt about its actual meaning, which is Ghosts – or in full, the Carriage of Ghosts. The constellation itself consists of four stars in a box shape, with a nebula in the centre, and clearly represents a chariot occupied by a ghostly spirit.

Yet the name 'Carriage of Ghosts' appears to be a recent invention – at least in Chinese historical terms. In recorded history, it seems that the nebula was picturesquely imagined to be the pollen blown from the willow-branches of the next mansion. Its symbolism, however, remained unchanged, as the Willow itself was associated with weeping and funeral rites.

Some idea of the malevolence which this mansion is deemed to possess can be gleaned from the fact that the Chinese character for 'Unlucky' is a representation of this very constellation.

The mansion Ghosts presides over departed spirits and funeral rites, cemeteries, and places where men have been killed, such as battlefields. As an extension to this, the mansion was also considered to preside over buried treasure, since it has ever been the custom to bury valuables for safe-keeping in times of war. The portents shown by this mansion are unfortunate.

Days which are ruled by Ghosts are unfavourable; any new projects will end in disaster. It is inadvisable to go through doors through which one has not passed before. Women who marry on a Ghosts day will be widows longer than wives. But prayers for the dead, memorial services, and visits to cemeteries to visit the tombs of ancestors will bring great merit and respect, and honours to one's own descendants.

Mansion 24 – The Willow

This is the companion to the preceding mansion, Ghosts, which in ancient times was thought to represent the pollen blown from the willow tree. Willow branches were borne in procession, especially at funeral rites, and thus the Willow is the symbol of tears.

It presides over vegetation.

Almost always, days which are ruled by the Willow are regarded as extremely inauspicious. No transactions are appropriate for such a day, and contrary to what might be expected, it is even regarded as unsuitable for funerals. Carelessness will be followed by discord, misdeeds by illness and harmful actions by ruin.

Mansion 25 – The Bird

The Bird Star, Alfard, is one of the two oldest recorded names of stars in Chinese astrology. It marks the Summer Solstice and as such is regarded as a bridge from the first half of the solar year to the second. Thus it came to preside over bridges and fords. But because robbers find bridges and passes ideal places to ambush the unwary traveller, it is taken to symbolize highway robbery, piracy and kidnapping.

As certain plants were gathered during the summer for making dyes, the mansion presides over textile dyeing, clothing and garments, pigments, paints and colours.

Days which are ruled by the Bird are ideally suited to building, and those who carry out construction work on a Bird day will gain promotion. But it is not an auspicious day for weddings or funerals; the woman who marries today will fall prey to a ravisher, and those who bury their dead today will see separation.

Mansion 26 – The Bow

The name of this mansion is taken from the shape of the constellation, which originally represented the spread wings of the Bird, and symbolizes the spreading out of a cloth, set out for a feast. Consequently it presides over festive occasions and celebrations, all the preparations beforehand, and all the events associated with celebrations such as the giving of presents, preparation of food, and even the kitchen and its utensils.

It reveals wealth at the end of a successful career. However, when the constellation was obscured, it was a bad omen, and a sign that the Emperor would fall ill. Consequently, when the sign is unfavourably aspected or occupied by an adverse star it portends sickness of the head of the family or of someone in authority.

Days which are ruled by the Bow are generally favourable. It shows thriving business, official success, the acquisition of new property, and happy personal relationships.

Mansion 27 – The Wings

This constellation was regarded as appearing at the time of the Grand Assembly at the Imperial Court, when the Emperor would read a report on the year's progress, followed by a grand performance of music and mime. Thus this mansion became associated with concerts of music, and the theatre. The numerous stars in this mansion represent the members of the imperial family and the court, and consequently the present-day meaning will refer to members of the ruling or legislative body of a nation.

Despite the fact that it presides over occasions of ceremony and pomp, the general indications of this mansion are unfavourable. It is regarded as portending chronic illness if it is adjacent to the House of Sickness.

Days which are ruled by the Wings are, for most events, unfortunate. Those who marry on a Wings day will suffer from chronic illness; men who leave home on business will return to find their wives in the arms of lovers. Nor is it an auspicious day to offer sacrifices to one's ancestors, as it foreshadows separation from one's own children, who will leave the country in later life.

Mansion 28 – The Carriage

Properly, the name of this mansion means the footboard of the carriage, but the interpretation derives from the image of the whole carriage.

Its original meaning was the bringing of tribute to the Emperor from far-off lands, and consequently it came to symbolize long journeys, and ultimately the vehicles which made those journeys. It presides over speed, travel and transport over land, and since this is the Palace of the Bird – it can be taken to include air transport.

Because the noise of carriages sounds like thunder (the Chinese name of this constellation is a homophone for thunder) it is the sign of a good wind for sailors. The passing of ths mansion denotes the end of a hurricane.

Its indications are favourable. It is regarded as the key to honour, recognition and promotion. However, if all five planets occur together in this mansion, it is a sign of war. Days which are ruled by the Carriage are auspicious for all kinds of mercantile business, and great profit will result. It is an ideal day for the landscape gardener, and if 'dragon terraces' are constructed it will bring the artisan and the owner great honour.

It is a favourable time to arrange obsequies and funeral rites for ancestors; and also for the contracting of marriages. Those who do either of these will find their own children developing rare talents, so bringing great honour to their parents.

Table XIV

Mansion	Element	Planet	Weather prospects	Trades and professions	Presides over	Adverse aspects
1 The Horn	Wood	Jupiter	Favourable winds and rains	Horticulture; agriculture	Growth; birth; marriage	Concluding affairs; funerals
2 The Neck	Water	Mercury	Extremes	Chemical industry	Judgments and punishments	Construction; marriages; funerals
3 The Base	Earth	Saturn	Strong rains, and winds	Flight; patent medicines	Correct actions	Travel by boat; marriage
4 The Room	—	Sun	Heat	Furnishers; decorators	Interiors of buildings	—
5 The Heart	—	Moon	—	Head of State	Imperial power	Ambitious plans
6 The Tail	Fire	Mars	—	Heir Apparent	Mothers; children; boats, dams; legacies	—
7 The Basket	Water	Mercury	—	Prosperity	New projects; burial	Slander; gossip
8 The Ladle	Wood	Jupiter	Rain; floods	Wine-merchants; oil; rewards	Digging; building	—
9 The Ox-Boy	Metal	Venus	—	Real estate	Roads, paths; land	Marriage
10 The Maiden	Earth	Saturn	—	Weaving	Property; dowry	Funerals
11 The Void	—	Sun	Rains and cold	Undertakers; frozen food	Cemeteries	Marriage

12 The Rooftop	Earth	Moon	—	Building	Fortification	Travel
13 The House	Fire	Mars	—	Religious orders	Physical work	—
14 The Wall	Water	Mercury	—	Literature; fine arts	Expansion; marriage	—
15 Astride	Wood	Jupiter	Cold	Footwear; textile processing	Clothing; armaments; canals	Building; digging
16 The Mound	Metal	Venus	Mildly cool and wet	Pharmacy	Festivities; symphonic music	—
17 The Stomach	Earth	Saturn	Floods	Banking	Investment; earthworks; marriage burial	Imprisonment
18 The Pleiades	—	Sun	—	Law	Judgments	Marriage; funerals; family reunions; digging; construction
19 The Net	—	Moon	Rains	Military	Hunting; marriage	Deserters; exile; frontiers
20 The Beak	Fire	Mars	—	Stock breeding	The infirm; flocks	Executions
21 Orion	Water	Mercury	—	Authorship	Labour	Completing tasks
22 The Well	Water	Jupiter	Rains	Civil Service; veterinary surgery	Widows; examinations	Delay, postponement; burial
23 Ghosts	Metal	Venus	—	—	Paying respects to the dead	—
24 The Willow	Earth	Saturn	—			—
25 The Bird	—	Sun	Heat	Garment industry	Dyestuffs; bridges	Marriages; funerals
26 The Bow	—	Moon	—	Theatre	Festivities; entertainment	—
27 Wings	Fire	Mars	—	Politics	Ceremonial	Marriage; funerals; leaving home
28 The Carriage	Water	Mercury	Wind; storms	Transport; landscape gardening	Travel, speed; marriage; digging; construction	—

5.

The Five Elements and the Five Planets

At the very core of Chinese philosophy lies the concept of the Five Elements – Wood, Fire, Earth, Metal, Water – which are believed to link all things in the universe. Their importance to astrology lies not just in the fact that no Chinese method of systematic thought can be divorced from the Five Element theory, but more pertinently, the five planets Mercury, Venus, Mars, Jupiter and Saturn are almost always known by the names of their element attributes.

Thus Mercury is the Water Star, Mars the Fire Star, Venus the Metal Star, Jupiter the Wood Star, and Saturn the Earth Star. Consequently, before dealing with the planets themselves, it is important to look at the Five Elements, their attributes, and the way in which they interact, since without an understanding of these basic principles, it would be impossible to grasp the relevance of the revelations of the Celestial Messengers.

The Five Cardinal Points

In the section on the Twenty-Eight Mansions, passing reference was made to the Elements in the section on the Four Palaces – North, West, South and East. The fifth element, Earth, belongs to the Centre, from which the other directions proceed. As a reminder, here is a summary of the relationships between the Elements, seasons and directions.

Jupiter	Wood – east – spring
Mars	Fire – south – summer
Saturn	Earth – centre – late summer
Venus	Metal – west – autumn
Mercury	Water – north – winter

Matters associated with a particular season also pertain to its direction and its relevant element, so that ultimately the symbolism of any one of the five planets can be traced to its associated direction and season. Jupiter for example, takes its portents from the east and the spring, and is thus the planet of birth and growth.

The symbolic meanings of the five planets are dealt with more fully in a later section (see page 83). But the interpretation of the Five Elements goes further than an understanding of the symbolism of each one individually. It is also important to realize the different ways in which the elements (or planets) interact, and the relation which each element has to the other four.

The Natural Production Sequence

Firstly, there is the natural or production order of the elements, which as we have seen, follow the seasons of the year.

Wood (burns, producing)
Fire (which leaves ash, or)
Earth (from which we extract)
Metal (which can melt to become like)
Water (which nourishes . . .)

The Production Order of the Five Elements

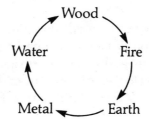

Thus in the production sequence, each element produces the next.

The Destruction Sequence

If the elements are taken alternately, this produces the destruction sequence, in which each element overpowers the next in order:

Wood eats Earth (draws nourishment from)
Earth drinks Water (absorbs or dirties it)
Water quenches Fire
Fire melts Metal
Metal chops Wood

The Destruction Order of the Five Elements

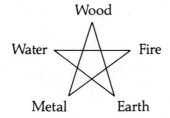

In the destruction sequence, each element destroys the next, but in quite different ways. It is interesting to examine the manner by which people representing each elemental quality may gain advantage over other types. The Wood type, drawing on the Earth type's resources, might be a constant emotional or financial drain; the Fire type would keep up a psychological attack (Fire usually representing intelligence) until the Metal type gave way; the Earth type would smirch the Water type's reputation; the Metal type would conquer Wood by direct attack; while the Water type would quench the Fire's enthusiasm and zeal.

Other Sequences

The diagram shows how the second sequence is derived from the first, in that in the second sequence, each second element is taken in turn.

It is possible to derive two further sequences of the five elements from that first one; that is by taking every third element in turn, and then every fourth. Taking every third element gives the sequence Wood–Metal–Fire–Water–Earth known as the 'mutually supporting series' and a moment's study will show that it is the reverse order of the Destruction Sequence.

If every fourth element is taken, the result (Water–Metal–Earth–Fire–Wood) is the reverse of the Natural Production Sequence. It is particularly interesting to astrologers because (reading the Earth element as the planet Earth instead of Saturn) it actually gives the order of the planets according to their distances from the Sun: Mercury, Venus, Earth, Mars, Jupiter (that is to say, the Water, Metal, Earth, Fire and Wood planets).

Supporting Planets

(a) Mutual Control

If any planets, represented by the elements in the horoscope, are found to be in an adverse

Mutual Control

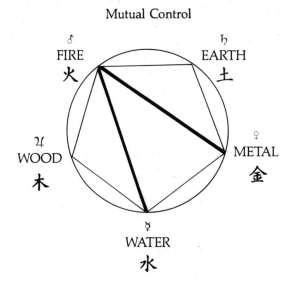

position, it is possible that other planets may counteract the unfavourable influences. For example, an element will not be destroyed by another if there is a third element in a position to destroy the second. This is called Mutual Control, because the 'destroying' element is controlled by the element which is produced by the element in the adverse position. A diagram makes this much easier to understand.

In this diagram, Metal would be destroyed by Fire (in Western astrological terms, Venus is unfavourably aspected by Mars) were it not for the fact that Fire is destroyed by Water (Mars is adversely aspected by Mercury), which is produced by Metal. Thus the three planets are balanced, and there is said to be 'mutual control'.

(b) Mutual Dissolution

There is another case in which unfavourable circumstances threatened by the adverse aspect of a planetary conjunction could be ameliorated.

If one element is badly aspected by another in the Destruction Sequence, then the presence of the intermediary element, which produces the badly aspected element, dissolves the adverse influences.

In the case above when Metal is under attack by Fire (Venus adversely aspected by Mars) if the intermediary element, Earth, is present, then the unfavourable aspects are neutralized. The following diagram will make this clear.

Mutual Dissolution

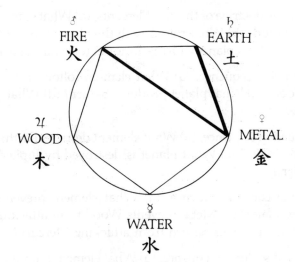

(c) Influence by Default

If four elements are present in one house, their adverse influences are all mutually controlled and dissolved. The element which is *not* present therefore has an 'influence by default'. That is to say, if four elements are present in an astrological Mansion or House, the most noticeable effect is that of the *negative* condition of the missing element.

For example, Wood represents creation, growth and expansion. If all four elements except Wood were present in a particular House or Mansion, then the prime interpretation must come from the fact that Wood is missing. Consequently, the most noticeable feature of that particular house would be its lack of growth and its inability to expand.

Negative influence by default

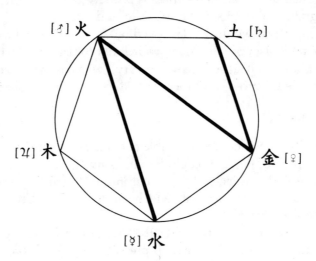

Readers may like to assess their understanding of the foregoing paragraphs by trying the following examples.

1. According to the doctrine of the Five Elements, (a) What season is associated with the element Wood? (b) What colour with the planet Jupiter? (c) What direction with White? (d) What planet with the Tortoise? (e) What element with the Centre?

2. In the production sequence, (a) What element follows Fire? (b) What element precedes Wood? (c) What planet produces Saturn? (d) What planet is produced by Mercury?

3. In the destruction sequence, (a) What element destroys Earth? (b) What element is destroyed by Fire? (c) What planet is destroyed by Jupiter? (d) What planet destroys Mars?

4. In the mutual control sequence, (a) What element prevents Fire from being quenched by Water? (b) Metal prevents Wood from attacking which element? (c) What planet prevents Saturn from attacking Mercury?

5. In the mutual dissolution sequence, (a) What element prevents Earth from soiling Water? (b) Mars stabilizes which two planets? (c) Venus and Jupiter are stabilized by which planet?

6. Jupiter, Mars, Saturn and Mercury are all present in one section of a Chinese horoscope. What should the astrologer note first of all?

Answers

1. (a) Spring,   (b) Green,   (c) West,   (d) Mercury, (e) Earth

2. (a) Earth,   (b) Water,   (c) Mars,   (d) Jupiter
3. (a) Wood,   (b) Metal,   (c) Saturn,   (d) Mercury
4. (a) Earth,   (b) Earth,   (c) Jupiter
5. (a) Metal   (b) Jupiter and Saturn,   (c) Mercury
6. The negative effect of Venus in default.

The Symbolism of the Five Planets

The symbolism of each planet is related to the season, colour and direction with which it is associated. An understanding of the symbolism of the directions gives a clear insight into the interpretation of the portents of the planets themselves. For this reason, this next section on the meaning of the planets is introduced by remarks on the directions. It is important not to overlook this section, in the mistaken belief that the directions have little to do with astrology, because in the Chinese system they are an integral function of it.

The skies are divided into Five Palaces; the Pole Star, and stars such as the constellation of the Great Bear which rotate round it, and are visible throughout the year, occupy the Purple Palace (encountered in the very first section of this book). The Sun, Moon and planets, however, never enter the Purple Palace and for this reason we can ignore it when discussing the auspices of the planets.

The four directional palaces are those of the Dragon (East), Bird (South), Tiger (West) and Tortoise (North). It is these which contain the twenty-eight lunar mansions, seven in each through which the planets travel.

The fifth direction is the Centre, representing the Earth, and by definition, there are no heavenly bodies in the Earth palace. However, the planet Saturn is known as the Earth planet, and its portents are taken from the symbolism of the element Earth, and the non-direction Centre.

There is yet another palace, the Jade-Green Palace, which includes the stars round the South Celestial Pole. Like the Purple Palace of the North Celestial Pole, the Jade Palace is another which is never visited by the Sun, Moon or planets, and for the purpose of planetary astrology, this too can be ignored. The six palaces can be imagined as the six faces of a cube projected onto a sphere, and their associated directions and planets can be summarized as follows.

The Purple Palace of the Crepe Myrtle
   Direction: celestial north. Season: none. Stars: the Great Bear and others. Element. none. Associated planet: none

The Green Palace of the Dragon
   Direction: East. Season: spring. Stars: Mansions 1–7. Element: Wood. Associated planet: Jupiter.

The Black Palace of the Tortoise
   Direction: north. Season: winter. Stars: Mansions 8–14. Element: Water. Associated planet: Mercury.

The Yellow Palace of the Emperor
  Direction: Centre. Season: late summer. Stars: none. Element: Earth. Associated planet: Saturn.

The White Palace of the Tiger
  Direction: west. Season: autumn. Stars: Mansions 15–21. Element: Metal. Associated planet: Venus.

The Red Palace of the Bird
  Direction: south. Season: summer. Stars: Mansions 22–28. Element: Fire. Associated planet: Mars.

The Jade Green Palace
  Direction: celestial south. Season: none. Stars: Southern Cross and others. Element: none. Associated planet: none.

The Eastern Direction – Ruled by Jupiter
Element: Wood
The time of the year ruled by the East is the spring, from 5 March onwards.

  The East is regarded as a fortunate direction. The Sun rises in the East, and so rules over new projects and new life. Consequently, it rules over childbirth and motherhood, and is the direction associated with the feminine.

  Thus its ruling planet, Jupiter, is the feminine planet (not Venus, which as we shall see, is the masculine planet). The East represents the enquirer, and matters pertaining to the enquirer's person, as distinct from family or relatives, and subjective interests.

  The Eastern Palace includes the first seven mansions from the Horn (of the Dragon) to the Basket. If more than one planet is present in Mansion 4 (the Room, signifying the Market Place) this indicates prosperity, the greater the number of planets, the greater the wealth. The second mansion, the Neck (which presides over illnesses, and is the first mansion to be mentioned in the *I Ching*) is the Temple, or favoured residence, of the Metal planet Venus, while the fifth mansion, the Heart, is the Temple of Mercury.

The Southern Direction – Ruled by Mars
Element: Fire
The time of the year ruled by the South is early summer, from 17 May.

  The South is regarded as an extremely fortunate direction, representing the Sun, the giver of life and energy, at its most powerful. It therefore represents power and prosperity. On the other hand, an excess of fire reveals drought, and burning – the actual dangers of physical fire.

  The Southern Palace includes the mansions 22 (the Well, the largest of the mansions) to 28 (the Carriage), and a non-mansional constellation called Heng, the Balance. If the Moon or planets pass through the southern palace in regular fashion, all bodes well. But if they appear to stop, this shows the death of a minister of State. Another non-mansional constellation mentioned in the ancient texts is the Harem.

  A text from the first century BC tells that when the Moon and planets maintain their position in the Harem (indicated by the star Regulus, which is in Leo) this has the same meaning as if they were together in the constellation of Heng (the Balance). The twenty-fifth mansion, the Bird, is the Temple of the Water planet, Mercury.

The Central Direction – Ruled by Saturn
Element: Earth
The time of the year ruled by the Centre is late summer, from 22 June.

The Centre pertains to terrestrial rather than celestial matters. It represents land, stability, resolution. Being stationary, it is the symbol of the immovable, and unchanging.

The Western Direction – Ruled by Venus
Element: Metal
The time of the year ruled by the West is autumn, from 3 September.

It therefore represents the setting sun, harvesting and wars, because after the harvesting, the soldiers could be employed in battle. The Western direction represents the masculine, and its ruling planet, Venus, is the masculine planet. (See the remarks above, under 'Eastern Direction'.)

Since the Eastern direction (q.v.) represents the Self, or the subjective, the Western direction represents the objective, and can mean opposition and conflict, and rivalry in partnership.

The Western palace includes the mansions 15 (Astride) to 21 (Orion).

The presence of Mars, the Fire planet, in the Western Palace indicates drought; if the Metal planet, Venus, is present, it reveals the threat of war, and if the Water planet, Mercury, is present, this indicates floods.

The Northern Direction – ruled by Mercury
Element: Water
The time of the year ruled by the North is winter, from 15 November.

The North represents cold, hibernation, stagnation, povery and loss. It is not regarded as an auspicious direction.

The Northern palace includes the mansions 8 (the Southern Ladle) to 14 (the Wall). If there are uprisings when the Fire planet, Mars, is in the North, it indicates that the army will be annihilated; but if the Metal planet (Venus) or Water planet (Mercury) is in the North, it means defeat but not total loss.

However, the presence of the Wood planet (Jupiter) or the Earth planet (Saturn) in the North is favourable.

When Mansion 12 (the Rooftop) is occupied by the Green or the Black planet (Jupiter, or Mercury) fish and salt become scarce.

Jupiter: The Year Star

Jupiter is known as the Wood planet. It rules over creation, birth, motherhood and creativity. For that reason, in Chinese astrology, Jupiter is said to be the planet of the feminine.

It is the ruling planet of the Spring mansions, 1–7, but its Temple, or 'domicile' is actually

Mansion 13, Ying Shih, the Burning House (or Temple of Sacrificial Fire).

Jupiter is known as the Year Star because it was from the progress of Jupiter through the heavens that the years of the twelve-year cycle (now known as the years of the Rat, Ox, Tiger, etc.) were reckoned. This system will be explained in greater detail later, in the section on the Twelve Jupiter Stations.

In the horoscope chart, Jupiter symbolizes virtuous love, and rules over the physical appearance.

Its negative aspects are coldness of heart, slovenly attitudes, and uncaring behaviour.

It is the symbol of happiness, and rules over agriculture and food. Jupiter is a fortunate planet, and when it progresses regularly, it shows happiness in the region associated with the mansion through which it passes.

If Jupiter is in its proper place, and all the other planets present, then there will be great prosperity in that region and the government will be stable.

If it is not in its proper place, and in Mansion 24, the Willow, there will be floods at first, and then drought.

When the planet Jupiter is found in a certain region, that is where the five grains prosper. If it misses its place, there will be harm to the regions it misses, but good to the regions where it stays.

If it is occulted (obscured) by the Moon, then a minister of State will be expelled.

When the Wood planet Jupiter is in advance or retardation, it determines the fate of the realm corresponding to the mansion in which it occurs. If it is in retardation, it reveals troubles for the region concerned. Because Jupiter is the symbol of the creative, no new projects should be initiated while it is in retardation.

When Mansion 12, the Rooftop, is occupied by the Green Planet (Jupiter), fish becomes scarce. But the Wood planet in the Northern Palace is favourable.

The spirit of Jupiter is depicted as a nobleman.

Mars: The Bright Fire

Mars is the Fire planet. Where it appears, in the corresponding Mansion there is war; when it disappears, soldiers can be given leave. In addition to war it signifies rebellion, piracy, illness, mourning and famine.

Mars symbolizes the ambassadors of countries.

Mars rules over the Southern Palace of Summer, mansions 22–28, but its Temple is the fifth mansion, Hsin, the Heart of the Dragon.

In the horoscope, Mars symbolizes courtesy, and rules over sight. But when negatively aspected, it shows rudeness, boorish behaviour, weak sight, and an inability to plan ahead.

It suggests pride, extravagance, upheavals, loss of order, and failure of the harvest.

Mars symbolizes the government and administration of the country. It forewarns of trouble for the Head of State when it enters the mansions 4, the Room, 5, the Heart (which is its own Temple), and 13, the Burning House (the Temple of Jupiter). If the Fire planet is in the Western Palace there will be droughts; if it retrogrades, there is calamity according to the magnitude of the retrogression. When it stops retrograding and goes direct, if calamities happen immediately, they will be soon over, no matter how great.

In the North, it signifies the death of a daughter, in the South, the death of a son.

If there are uprisings in the Northern Palace when Mars is present in the corresponding mansion, the army will be annihilated.

When Mars is in close conjunction with other planets, it indicates a disaster, and the closer the planets are, the greater the calamity will be.

In Mansion 13, it reveals evil to the Head of State. If Venus and Mars halt at the mid-point of the Southern Palace, it means common people are rising and plotting.

The spirit of the Fire Planet is depicted as a youth.

Saturn: The Regulator

Saturn is the Earth planet. The realm over which it rules is fortunate. Although, as in the West, the Spirit of Saturn is portrayed as an old man, the Chinese symbolism of the Earth planet has none of the gloomy portents associated with it in the Western world. On the contrary, it is frequently alluded to as a bringer of happiness and long life.

It rules the Central Direction, that is, the planet Earth. Its Temple is the Southern Ladle, the eighth mansion.

In the horoscope, Saturn symbolizes truthfulness, and rules over intelligence. Because it rules the Centre, it rules over the four planets, and as truth conquers calumny, and intelligence overrides ignorance, so Saturn can outshine the other planets when they are malevolently aspected.

It signifies safety, but when adversely aspected, danger.

If it returns to a region after retrogression, or retrogresses back to a region, there will be good fortune in the affairs of that region. The region will gain territory and women. But as to the region where Saturn is now missing, the associated nation will lose territory, and harm will fall upon its womenfolk.

When Saturn remains in a mansion for an unusually long period, it indicates that the corresponding realm will be happy and prosperous. But when it moves quickly away from a region, happiness is lost.

If it is in advance and travelling quickly through three mansions, it shows that government legislation is not being carried out and the people will suffer; if it is in retardation, its progress being delayed over three mansions, the country's womenfolk from the Queen to the lowliest widow will grieve over their condition. Furthermore, Saturn in retardation means a poor harvest, earthquakes, and other disasters connected with the land.

Venus: The Great White

Venus is the Metal planet. Because it is associated with Metal, representing swords and armour, the planet Venus is regarded as the masculine planet – the very converse of Western astrological symbolism. Its companion – the feminine planet – is Jupiter, so explaining the name of the conjunction of Venus and Jupiter, 'male and female' – Venus, in this case, being the masculine planet.

Venus rules the Western Palace of Autumn, mansions 15–21. Its temple is the second mansion, the Neck of the Dragon. When present there, Venus represents the Prime Minister.

In the horoscope, Venus symbolizes honest dealings, and rules over speech. Consequently, when it retrogresses, it signifies dishonesty, secret deals and espionage.

If Venus is found near the Moon, it indicates an attempted military coup. If in close conjunction with Jupiter, there will be battles in the region associated with the mansion where the conjunction takes place. (This is known as the *male and female* conjunction.)

If Venus, the planet of war, is not in evidence when soldiers are sent out, the army will be restive, and morale low. When Venus appears south of Mao (Branch IV representing the Eastern horizon), or north of Yü (Branch X representing the West) the South vanquishes the North; in Mao itself, victory is in the East; in Yü, in the West. (These terms are further explained in the section on the Jupiter stations. See page 85.)

When Venus comes into contact with any celestial body, it indicates battles. The direction of the celestial body which comes into contact with Venus reveals the direction of the losing side.

Generally speaking, if Venus is in the east, this is favourable, the unfavourable aspects of Venus, the western planet, being counterbalanced by the more fortunate east direction. Conversely, when Venus is in the west, this indicates conflict.

If Venus is occulted (i.e. hidden – eclipsed) by the Moon, there is strife. However, should Venus be visible in daylight, or at midday, this is called 'Unrivalled Brightness' and shows prosperity and change.

The spirit of the Metal Planet (Venus) is depicted as a lumberjack.

Mercury: The Water Planet

Chinese astrologers of ancient times had many different names for Mercury, which gives the main clue to its symbolism. It was known as the Little Regulator (Saturn was the Great Regulator); the Celestial Support; the Peaceful Surround; the Delicate and Brisk (on account of the planet's size and speed) and the Hook.

Mercury is associated with the Northern Palace, mansions 8–14. Its Temple is the twenty-fifth mansion, the Bird Star; when present it represents the Celestial Registrar or Historian. It symbolizes judges and trials.

In the horoscope, Mercury symbolizes knowledge, and rules over hearing. But when adversely aspected, it indicates lack of common sense, a refusal to listen to reason, and defects in hearing and communications.

If it appears on the boundary between Mansion 4 (the Room) and Mansion 5 (the Heart) it warns of earthquakes. When Mansion 12, the Rooftop, is occupied by the Black Planet (Mercury), salt becomes scarce.

When Mercury and Venus appear in the East, foreign powers are vanquished and the Middle Kingdom is victorious. When Mercury and Venus appear in the West, a foreign power will be victorious. If Mercury appears in the East when Venus is in the West, or in the West when Venus is in the East, there will be discord, but no battle. (But note that as Venus and Mercury are never more than 76° apart, the text probably means a few degrees west and east of the meridian respectively.)

If Mercury and Venus appear in a Mansion corresponding to a country which is at war, unless there is another planet present, there will be no battle.

When Mercury is to the North of Venus, the army will be defeated and the general killed. If it appears to the South of Venus, the foreign army will lose territory.

If Mercury moves towards Venus, which remains stationary, then a general will die.

The spirit of the Water Planet (Mercury) is depicted as a woman.

The Moon

The Moon is the essence of the Great Yin, or recessive flux. It is the counterpart of the Sun and represents the Empress. Its coolness symbolizes calm and peace, but when adversely aspected it denotes punishments.

Repeated appearances of the Moon by day indicate vice, cruelty, disagreement, confusion and the downfall of the state.

Matters revealed by the Moon usually refer to the people of a state, as distinct from the Sun, which symbolizes the rulers or government.

When the Moon passes through the Horn (Mansion 1) in the autumn, the spring floods will occur six months later. If the Moon is eclipsed in the Room (Mansion 4) it indicates the death of a minister of State.

Occultations by the Moon

If the Moon occults (obscures) Jupiter, then the region corresponding to the Mansion in which the occultation occurs will face ruin and starvation.

If the Moon occults Mars, there will be revolutions and uprisings.

If it occults Saturn, there will be mutinies and insubordination.

If it occults Venus, a powerful state will lose a battle.

If it occults Mercury, there will be troubles connected with women.

Eclipses of the Sun and Moon

Eclipses are not good omens. Those of the Sun concern the ruler or government of the country; those of the Moon concern the people.

Ancient texts confidently assert that eclipses occurring on the days of stem 1 and 2, which are governed by Wood (Jupiter) denote events occurring beyond the four seas, and can therefore be ignored. Today, such regions would be the trans-Pacific regions of the North and South Americas.

Similarly, on days 3 and 4, governed by Fire (Mars) eclipses concern South-East Asia.

On days 5 and 6, governed by Earth (Saturn), they concern China and India.

On days 7 and 8, governed by Metal (Venus) they concern Africa.

On days 9 and 10, governed by Water (Mercury), they concern the Soviet Union and Europe.

General Remarks

If a planet is accelerating, this is known as being in advance; when a planet advances, it is called the 'guest'. Its portents do not affect the person whose horoscope is being cast directly, but rather, someone who is close to the subject. Conversely, when there are indications pertaining to family or others, but the planet is retarding, this indicates events which pertain to the subject rather than another. When five planets appear together in the same lunar mansion, this is called 'Changing Elements'. A new leader will come to power [in the country corresponding to the lunar mansion]. Those who are virtuous will prosper, but those who are not upright will come to disaster.

Conjunctions

In Western astrology, great importance is attached to the angles made between the positions of two planets in a horoscope. In ancient China, as can be seen from the astrologers' manuals, the planetary conjunctions were studied in order to discover the likelihood of success in military campaigns. The function of the Imperial astrologer was, more than anything else, to ascertain which regions were likely to be insurgent, so that the armies could be despatched in good time to the locations where they would most likely be needed. The following summary of the conjunctions in the classical texts is given not just out of historical interest, since it is expected to appeal strongly to those astrologers – and others – who specialize in predicting world events. However, in order to give these aspects a wider application, a parallel interpretation for modern-day use is also given. *To keep the precepts taken from the ancient texts clearly distinct, the modern interpretations have been given in italics.*

The order of the conjunctions listed here follows the production order of the Five Elements – Wood, Fire, Earth, Metal, Water – or in other words, Jupiter, Mars, Saturn, Venus, Mercury.

Conjunctions formed with the Wood Planet (Jupiter)

Wood/Fire

The ancient texts give no prognostications for the conjunction of Jupiter and Mars.

These two planets are in the production sequence. As Wood represents creativity, and Fire rebellion, this indicates a highly creative talent of an extremely original nature. But as Fire consumes Wood, it indicates the wasting of resources. If the conjunction occurs in the House of Sickness, then it indicates childhood illness.

Wood/Earth

The Wood planet and the Earth planet indicate problems within the state; wood and earth signifies vegetation in the earth, without fire or water, so revealing famine. It reveals that the leader of a state will wage war unexpectedly and be vanquished.

The presence of these two normally beneficial planets in the same mansion is, strangely, not a fortunate sign; it reveals absence of purpose. Stubbornness and lack of resources lead to stagnation, and an inability to put ideas into practice.

However, if the conjunction takes place in the northern part of the horoscope, that is, near the midnight segment, it shows that in the case of an unexpected confrontation or civil lawsuit, the other party will be unsuccessful.

Wood/Metal

When the Wood planet is in opposition to the Metal planet, the army of the corresponding region is destroyed.

When the Wood planet is in conjunction with the Metal planet, there will be battles in the corresponding region. (This is known as the 'male and female' conjunction.)

If Jupiter is in the opposite mansion to Venus (see Horoscope Workchart II) this is beneficial, as it indicates that opposition to plans will be overcome.

If Jupiter and Venus are in the same mansion, there will be problems in the corresponding House of the horoscope.

Wood/Water

The ancient texts give no interpretation of the Jupiter and Mercury conjunction.

Jupiter and Mercury represent Wood and Water; nothing could be more propitious for the growth and expansion of business. It shows success in all fields, prosperity and health.

Conjunctions formed with the Fire Planet (Mars)

Fire/Wood: see Wood/Fire.

Fire/Earth

The Fire planet and the Earth planet together indicate drought. There is sorrow. It is unlucky for public officials; the people will suffer famine; enterprises are unsuccessful.

There are resources and ideas, but there are difficulties in communication, whether the physical transport of resources, or the inability to get new ideas accepted. It reveals frustrations at the lack of flexibility.

Those in administration or public office will have to face unexpected difficulties in adverse circumstances, such as those brought on by natural disasters.

Fire/Metal

The Fire planet and the Metal planet together indicate mourning. If the Fire planet and the Metal planet halt in the middle position of the Southern Palace (that is, in Hsiu 25, the Bird) this indicates insubordination, and the masses rising and plotting.

The conjunction of Mars and Venus was regarded unfavourably by the ancient Chinese, as it was held to forebode the death of a relative. If the conjunction appears at the noon position in the horoscope, it will reveal difficulties in dealing with subordinates. Such a person will find it difficult to achieve success in a managerial capacity unless diplomacy can be used where confrontation might be otherwise expected.

Fire/Water

The Fire planet and the Water planet together indicate famine.

The conjunction of Mars and Mercury shows fire boiling water, but the steam is generating nothing. It shows considerable effort, but without result. The Chinese symbol for 'catastrophe' consists of the two characters for water and fire together, thus suggesting that the appearance of these two planets in the same mansion indicates a calamity pertaining to that mansion or the House in which it stands.

Conjunctions formed with the Earth Planet (Saturn)

Earth/Wood: see Wood/Earth.

Earth/Fire: see Fire/Earth.

Earth/Metal

The Metal planet in the same mansion as the Earth planet indicates bereavement, epidemics, civil wars, and loss of territory.

The conjunction of Saturn, representing the Earth, or territory, with the metal of Venus, signifying a sword, shows land being cut off. It would be an unfortunate conjunction in the House of Land and Dwelling, as it would indicate the selling of property and the loss of land. In the House of Sickness, or any of the houses representing family, it would indicate illness or bereavement.

Earth/Water

The Earth planet in conjunction with the Water planet indicates a change of policy; there is prosperity, but obstacles in the way of complete satisfaction. New enterprises are marked by hindrances; it would be foolish to embark on any campaign which attempted to defeat a nation which was benignly watched over by the Earth planet.

The auspices shown by Saturn and Mercury are very mixed, and generally unhelpful. Earth sullies Water, which shows the spoiling of communications, while Water washes away the firm resolve – the usual interpretation of Earth. More positively, earth and water together make clay, which shows real-estate. The signs are of someone torn between staying in one place (shown by Saturn, the Earth planet) and travel (revealed by Mercury, the Water planet). It would be much better for such a person to invest in two residences.

Earth + two other planets

The Earth planet in conjunction with two other planets in the same mansion indicates revolution and change. In such a case the Earth planet becomes dominant, and is able to conquer the adverse aspects of the other two planets.

The conjunction of Saturn with two other planets in the same mansion is extremely favourable, for it shows the subjugation of any of the adverse influences of the other two planets, and the heightening of their positive aspects. So wherever the conjunction of the other planets bodes unfavourably, the meaning must be reversed to give a positive and beneficial interpretation.

Earth + three other planets

The conjunction of the Earth planet with three other planets is not beneficial; rather, it indicates wars and bereavements. Highly placed people become afflicted, while lesser men are led to becoming criminals.

Conversely, however, the conjunction of Saturn with three other planets is decidedly adverse, indicating unfavourable circumstances. The interpretation must be taken from the planet in default.

Conjunctions formed with the Metal Planet (Venus)

Metal/Wood: see Wood/Metal.

Metal/Fire: see Fire/Metal.

Metal/Earth: see Earth/Metal.

Metal/Water
When the Water planet and the Metal planet appear in the east, foreign powers are vanquished and the Middle Kingdom is victorious. When the Water planet and the Metal planet appear in the west, a foreign power will be victorious.

If the Water planet appears in the east when the Metal planet is in the west, or in the west when the Metal planet is in the east, there will be discord, but no battle.

If the Water planet and the Metal planet appear in a mansion corresponding to a country which is at war, unless there is another planet present, there will be no battle.

When the Water planet is to the north of the Metal planet, the army will be defeated and the general killed. If it appears to the south of the Metal planet, the foreign army will lose territory.

If the Water planet moves towards the Metal planet, which does not move away, then a general will die.

When Mercury and Venus appear together in the east, it shows the surmounting of difficulties, and reveals obstacles being overcome. But if the conjunction appears in the west of the horoscope chart, the outcome is not favourable.

If Venus and Mercury are in mansions on opposite sides of the horoscope on an east–west axis, this reveals obstacles and difficulties, but they will be overcome, although no progress will be made.

If there is a conjunction of Mercury and Venus in a mansion or house corresponding to some difficulty being experienced at the time, then the difficulties will eventually pass. For example, if there was a question regarding health, and Venus and Mercury appeared in the Sickness and Health mansion, it would show eventual recovery from illness.

If Mercury is placed north of Venus in the horoscope, this is unfavourable; it shows conflict in the corresponding house; but if Venus is north of Mercury, this is fortunate; if there are difficulties, these will be resolved.

Metal/Moon
When the Metal planet and the Moon appear close together, it indicates that a general will become flushed with pride.

If Mercury and the Moon appear close, but not in occultation, and not necessarily in the same mansion, it indicates insubordination. The closer the two bodies, the greater will be the difficulties. In the House of Servants and Slaves, it would indicate trouble in business and management. For those not in business, or if the conjunction appeared in the House of Sons and Daughters, it would signify rebelliousness in children.

Conjunctions formed with the Water Planet

Water/Wood: see Wood/Water.

Water/Fire: see Fire/Water.

Water/Earth: see Water/Earth.

Water/Metal: see Metal/Water.

6.

More about the Chinese Calendar

Earlier, we looked at the way that Chinese astrologers of old established the Moon's position. This method gave a fairly good approximation, and had the advantage of using only the two calendars for the data. Of course, Chinese astrologers would not have used the Western calendar to establish the Sun's position; indeed they already had a 'solar calendar' of their own.

The solar calendar consists of twenty-four virtually equal divisions of the solar year, called in Chinese *Ch'i* or 'breaths'. As each breath is therefore just over fifteen days long, they can reasonably be called 'fortnights'. (The term is one which British and French readers would perhaps be more familiar with – 'fortnight' literally means 'fourteen nights', and the French *quinzaine* 'fifteen days'!)

As each fortnight is a division of the solar year, it follows that each fortnight is actually a division of the *ecliptic* – which is, by definition, the Sun's apparent path through the sky. The twenty-four fortnights are paired into twelve *Chieh*, or 'festivals'. Since these twelve 'festivals' divide the ecliptic into twelve, they would be the exact equivalent of the Western zodiacal signs but for one thing – the Chinese propensity to reckon time by the *mid-points* of periods, rather than the beginnings. As a consequence, each of the twelve festivals is actually the latter half of one sign, and the beginning half of the next.

The following table will make this evident.

Table XV: The Twenty-Four Ch'i

立春	1.	Li Ch'un	Spring commences	Midpoint of Aquarius
雨水	2.	Yü Shui	Rain water	Sun enters Pisces
驚蟄	3.	Ching Chih	Insects waken	Midpoint of Pisces
春分	4.	Ch'un Fen	Spring Equinox	Sun enters Aries
清明	5.	Ch'ing Ming	Clear and Bright	Midpoint of Aries
穀雨	6.	Ku Yu	Corn Rain	Sun enters Taurus
立夏	7.	Li Hsia	Summer commences	Midpoint of Taurus
小滿	8.	Hsiao Man	Corn sprouting	Sun enters Gemini
芒種	9.	Mang Chung	Corn in ear	Midpoint of Gemini

夏至	10.	Hsia Chih	Summer Solstice	Sun enters Cancer
小暑	11.	Hsiao Shu	Little Heat	Midpoint of Cancer
大暑	12.	Ta Shu	Great Heat	Sun enters Leo
立秋	13.	Li Ch'iu	Autumn commences	Midpoint of Leo
處暑	14.	Ch'u Shu	Heat finishes	Sun enters Virgo
白露	15.	Pai Lu	White Dew	Midpoint of Virgo
秋分	16.	Ch'iu Fen	Autumn Equinox	Sun enters Libra
寒露	17.	Han Lu	Cold Dew	Midpoint of Libra
霜降	18.	Shuang Chiang	Frost descends	Sun enters Scorpio
立冬	19.	Li Tung	Winter commences	Midpoint of Scorpio
小雪	20.	Hsiao Hsüeh	Little Snow	Sun enters Sagittarius
大雪	21.	Ta Hsüeh	Great Snow	Midpoint of Sagittarius
冬至	22.	Thung Chih	Winter Solstice	Sun enters Capricorn
小寒	23.	Hsiao Han	Little cold	Midpoint of Capricorn
大寒	24.	Ta Han	Great Cold	Sun enters Aquarius

These solar terms are of great importance to the Chinese astrologer when calculating a horoscope, since they define the Sun's position along the ecliptic. As we have seen already, however, the same function is performed by the Western calendar, and for most purposes, we can ignore the solar terms and instead refer to ephemerides and almanacs using the Western date. Some aspects of certain Chinese astrological calculations, however, depend on a precise definition of the solar term for the calculations.

As an example of their use, the next worksheet explains the method for calculating the Twelve indicators, sometimes called the 'clothes-cutting days' on account of the fact that in the old texts, the first day to be listed was deemed to be suitable for cutting out clothes.

These days are clearly marked in almanacs of the present day, and have a ritual – almost religious – significance to orthodox Chinese who regulate their working lives by the precepts of the 'clothes-cutting' days.

Most Chinese astrologers reckon the allotted span of life from the lunar and solar calendars, and for them it is important to determine the dates of the festivals with some accuracy. Therefore, as the dates of solar phenomena vary slightly from year to year, the dates for the commencement of each of the twenty-four Ch'i for the present century are given in Table XVI.

The Twelve Indicators

The Twelve Indicators are known to the Chinese as the *Chien-Ch'ü* simply because *Chien* and *Ch'ü* are the names of the first two characters in the system. They reveal the actions best suited to the day in question. The Indicator for the day can be found very simply by cross-referring the Branch of the Day with the Monthly Festival in Table XVII. More precise instructions are given in Worksheet 5.

Table XVII: To find the Indicator for the Day

DAY BRANCH:		I	II	III	IV	V	VI	VII	VIII	IX	X	XI	XII
from/to *	Ch'i												
Dec. 7	21	A	B	C	D	E	F	G	H	I	J	K	L
Jan. 6	23	L	A	B	C	D	E	F	G	H	I	J	K
Feb. 4	1	K	L	A	B	C	D	E	F	G	H	I	J
Mar. 6	3	J	K	L	A	B	C	D	E	F	G	H	I
Apr. 5	5	I	J	K	L	A	B	C	D	E	F	G	H
May. 6	7	H	I	J	K	L	A	B	C	D	E	F	G
Jun. 6	9	G	H	I	J	K	L	A	B	C	D	E	F
Jul. 8	11	F	G	H	I	J	K	L	A	B	C	D	E
Aug. 8	13	E	F	G	H	I	J	K	L	A	B	C	D
Sep. 8	15	D	E	F	G	H	I	J	K	L	A	B	C
Oct. 9	17	C	D	E	F	G	H	I	J	K	L	A	B
Nov. 8	19	B	C	D	E	F	G	H	I	J	K	L	A

*Approximate dates. If the date in question is close to one of the dates in the column, check with those given in Table XVI.

The year of twenty-four fortnights begins on either 4 or 5 February. Consequently, the twenty-third and twenty-fourth fortnights ('Little Cold' and 'Great Cold') both begin in January. In the table, the figures in the columns give the dates of the Western months on which the fortnights commence. Thus in 1900, 'Little Cold' began on 6 January, 'Great Cold' on 20 January, and 'Spring Commences' (the first fortnight) on 6 February.

The twelve festivals begin with the first fortnight of each Western month, always between the 4th and the 9th of the month; this simplifies looking up the dates of the twelve festivals in the table, as they always begin on a single-figure date.

Table XVI: Dates of the Twenty-Four Ch'i for Years AD 1900 to 2000

Ch'i	23	24	1	2	3	4	5	6	7	8	9	10	11	12	13	14	15	16	17	18	19	20	21	22
					EQUINOX						SOLSTICE						EQUINOX						SOLSTICE	
Year	Jan		Feb		Mar		Apr		May		Jun		Jul		Aug		Sep		Oct		Nov		Dec	
1900	6	20	4	19	6	21	5	20	6	21	6	22	7	23	8	23	8	23	9	24	8	23	7	22
1901	6	21	4	19	6	21	5	21	6	22	6	22	8	23	8	24	8	24	9	24	8	23	8	22
1902	6	21	5	19	6	21	6	21	6	22	7	22	8	24	8	24	8	24	9	24	8	23	8	23
1903	6	21	5	20	7	22	6	21	7	22	7	22	8	24	9	24	9	24	9	24	8	23	8	23
1904	7	21	5	20	6	21	5	20	6	21	6	22	7	23	8	23	8	23	9	24	8	23	7	22
1905	6	21	4	19	6	21	5	21	6	22	6	22	8	23	8	24	8	24	9	24	8	23	8	22
1906	6	21	5	19	6	21	6	21	6	22	6	22	8	24	8	24	8	24	9	24	8	23	8	23
1907	6	21	5	20	7	22	6	21	7	22	7	22	8	24	9	24	9	24	9	24	8	23	8	23
1908	7	21	5	20	6	21	5	20	6	21	6	22	7	23	8	23	8	23	9	24	8	23	7	22
1909	6	21	4	19	6	21	5	21	6	22	6	22	8	23	8	24	8	24	9	24	8	23	8	22
1910	6	21	5	19	6	21	6	21	6	22	6	22	8	24	8	24	8	24	9	24	8	23	8	23
1911	6	21	5	20	7	22	6	21	7	22	7	22	8	24	9	24	9	24	9	24	8	23	8	23
1912	7	21	5	20	6	21	5	20	6	21	6	22	7	23	8	23	8	23	9	24	8	23	7	22
1913	6	20	4	19	6	21	5	21	6	22	6	22	8	23	8	24	8	24	9	24	8	23	8	22
1914	6	21	4	19	6	21	5	21	6	22	6	22	8	24	8	24	8	24	9	24	8	23	8	23
1915	6	21	5	20	6	22	6	21	6	22	7	22	8	24	8	24	9	24	9	24	8	23	8	23
1916	6	21	5	20	6	21	5	20	6	21	6	22	7	23	8	23	8	23	8	24	8	22	7	22
1917	6	20	4	19	6	21	5	21	6	21	6	22	8	23	8	24	8	23	9	24	8	23	7	22
1918	6	21	4	19	6	21	5	21	6	22	6	22	8	24	8	24	8	24	9	24	8	23	8	22
1919	6	21	5	20	6	22	6	21	6	22	7	22	8	24	8	24	9	24	9	24	8	23	8	23
1920	6	21	5	20	6	21	5	20	6	21	6	22	7	23	8	23	8	23	8	24	8	22	7	22
1921	6	20	4	19	6	21	5	20	6	21	6	22	8	23	8	24	8	23	9	24	8	23	7	22
1922	6	21	4	19	6	21	5	21	6	22	6	22	8	24	8	24	8	24	9	24	8	23	8	22
1923	6	21	5	19	6	21	6	21	6	22	7	22	8	24	8	24	9	24	9	24	8	23	8	23
1924	6	21	5	20	6	21	5	20	6	21	6	22	7	23	8	23	8	23	8	24	8	22	7	22
1925	6	20	4	19	6	21	5	20	6	21	6	22	8	23	8	24	8	23	9	24	8	23	7	22
1926	6	21	4	19	6	21	5	21	6	22	6	22	8	23	8	24	8	24	9	24	8	23	8	22
1927	6	21	5	19	6	21	6	21	6	22	7	22	8	24	8	24	8	24	9	24	8	23	8	23
1928	6	21	5	20	6	21	5	20	6	21	6	21	7	23	8	23	8	23	8	23	7	22	7	22
1929	6	20	4	19	6	21	5	20	6	21	6	22	7	23	8	23	8	23	9	24	8	23	7	22
1930	6	21	4	19	6	21	5	21	6	22	6	22	8	23	8	24	8	24	9	24	8	23	8	22
1931	6	21	5	20	6	21	6	21	6	22	7	22	8	24	8	24	8	24	9	24	8	23	8	23
1932	6	21	5	20	6	21	5	20	6	21	6	21	7	23	8	23	8	23	8	23	7	22	7	22
1933	6	20	4	19	6	21	5	20	6	21	6	22	7	23	8	23	8	23	9	24	8	23	7	22
1934	6	21	4	19	6	21	5	21	6	22	6	22	8	23	8	24	8	24	9	24	8	23	8	22
1935	6	21	5	19	6	21	6	21	6	22	6	22	8	24	8	24	8	24	9	24	8	23	8	23
1936	6	21	5	20	6	21	5	20	6	21	6	21	7	23	8	23	8	23	8	23	7	22	7	22
1937	6	20	4	19	6	21	5	20	6	21	6	22	7	23	8	23	8	23	9	24	8	23	7	22
1938	6	21	4	19	6	21	5	21	6	22	6	22	8	23	8	24	8	24	9	24	8	23	8	22
1939	6	21	5	19	6	21	6	21	6	22	6	22	8	24	8	24	8	24	9	24	8	23	8	23

Ch'i	23	24	1	2	3	4	5	6	7	8	9	10	11	12	13	14	15	16	17	18	19	20	21	22
Year	Jan		Feb		Mar (EQUINOX)		Apr		May		Jun (SOLSTICE)		Jul		Aug		Sep (EQUINOX)		Oct		Nov		Dec (SOLSTICE)	
1940	6	21	5	20	6	21	5	20	6	21	6	21	7	23	8	23	8	23	8	23	7	22	7	22
1941	6	20	4	19	6	21	5	20	6	21	6	22	7	23	8	23	8	23	9	24	8	23	7	22
1942	6	21	4	19	6	21	5	21	6	22	6	22	8	23	8	24	8	24	9	24	8	23	8	22
1943	6	21	5	19	6	21	6	21	6	22	6	22	8	24	8	24	8	24	9	24	8	23	8	23
1944	6	21	5	20	6	21	5	20	5	21	6	21	7	23	8	23	8	23	8	23	7	22	7	22
1945	6	20	4	19	6	21	5	20	6	21	6	22	7	23	8	23	8	23	8	24	8	22	7	22
1946	6	20	4	19	6	21	5	21	6	22	6	22	8	23	8	24	8	23	9	24	8	23	8	22
1947	6	21	4	19	6	21	5	21	6	22	6	22	8	24	8	24	8	24	9	24	8	23	8	23
1948	6	21	5	20	5	21	5	20	5	21	6	21	7	23	7	23	8	23	8	23	7	22	7	22
1949	5	20	4	19	6	21	5	20	6	21	6	22	7	23	8	23	8	23	8	24	8	22	7	22
1950	6	20	4	19	6	21	5	20	6	21	6	22	8	23	8	24	8	23	9	24	8	23	8	22
1951	6	21	4	19	6	21	5	21	6	22	6	22	8	24	8	24	8	24	9	24	8	23	8	23
1952	6	21	5	20	5	21	5	20	5	21	6	21	7	23	7	23	8	23	8	23	7	22	7	22
1953	5	20	4	19	6	21	5	20	6	21	6	22	7	23	8	23	8	23	8	24	8	22	7	22
1954	6	20	4	19	6	21	5	20	6	21	6	22	8	23	8	24	8	23	9	24	8	23	7	22
1955	6	21	4	19	6	21	5	21	6	22	6	22	8	23	8	24	8	24	9	24	8	23	8	22
1956	6	21	5	20	5	20	5	20	5	21	6	21	7	23	7	23	8	23	8	23	7	22	7	22
1957	5	20	4	19	6	21	5	20	6	21	6	22	7	23	8	23	8	23	8	24	8	22	7	22
1958	6	20	4	19	6	21	5	20	6	21	6	22	7	23	8	23	8	23	9	24	8	23	7	22
1959	6	21	4	19	6	21	5	21	6	22	6	22	8	23	8	24	8	24	9	24	8	23	8	22
1960	6	21	5	19	5	20	5	20	5	21	6	21	7	23	7	23	7	23	8	23	7	22	7	22
1961	5	20	4	19	6	21	5	20	6	21	6	21	7	23	8	23	8	23	8	23	7	22	7	22
1962	6	20	4	19	6	21	5	20	6	21	6	22	7	23	8	23	8	23	9	24	8	23	7	22
1963	6	21	4	19	6	21	5	21	6	22	6	22	8	23	8	24	8	24	9	24	8	23	8	22
1964	6	21	5	19	5	20	5	20	5	21	6	21	7	23	7	23	7	23	8	23	7	22	7	22
1965	5	20	4	19	6	21	5	20	6	21	6	21	7	23	8	23	8	23	8	23	7	22	7	22
1966	6	20	4	19	6	21	5	20	6	21	6	22	7	23	8	23	8	23	9	24	8	23	7	22
1967	6	21	4	19	6	21	5	21	6	22	6	22	8	23	8	24	8	24	9	24	8	23	8	22
1968	6	21	5	19	5	20	5	20	5	21	5	21	7	23	7	23	7	23	8	23	7	22	7	22
1969	5	20	4	19	6	21	5	20	6	21	6	21	7	23	8	23	8	23	8	23	7	22	7	22
1970	6	20	4	19	6	21	5	20	6	21	6	22	7	23	8	23	8	23	9	24	8	23	7	22
1971	6	21	4	19	6	21	5	21	6	22	6	22	8	23	8	24	8	24	9	24	8	23	8	22
1972	6	21	5	19	5	20	5	20	5	21	5	21	7	23	7	23	7	23	8	23	7	22	7	22
1973	5	20	4	19	6	21	5	20	5	21	6	21	7	23	8	23	8	23	8	23	7	22	7	22
1974	6	20	4	19	6	21	5	20	6	21	6	22	7	23	8	23	8	23	9	24	8	23	7	22
1975	6	21	4	19	6	21	5	21	6	22	6	22	8	23	8	24	8	23	9	24	8	23	8	22
1976	6	21	5	19	5	20	4	20	5	21	5	21	7	23	7	23	7	23	8	23	7	22	7	22
1977	5	20	4	19	6	21	5	20	5	21	6	21	7	23	7	23	8	23	8	23	7	22	7	22
1978	6	20	4	19	6	21	5	20	6	21	6	22	7	23	8	23	8	23	8	24	8	23	7	22
1979	6	21	4	19	6	21	5	21	6	21	6	22	8	23	8	24	8	23	9	24	8	23	8	22
1980	6	21	5	19	5	20	4	20	5	21	5	21	7	23	7	23	7	23	8	23	7	22	7	22
1981	5	20	4	19	6	21	5	20	5	21	6	21	7	23	7	23	8	23	8	23	7	22	7	22

Ch'i	23	24	1	2	3	4	5	6	7	8	9	10	11	12	13	14	15	16	17	18	19	20	21	22
					EQUINOX						SOLSTICE						EQUINOX						SOLSTICE	
Year	Jan		Feb		Mar		Apr		May		Jun		Jul		Aug		Sep		Oct		Nov		Dec	
1982	6	20	4	19	6	21	5	20	6	21	6	22	7	23	8	23	8	23	8	24	8	22	7	22
1983	6	20	4	19	6	21	5	20	6	21	6	22	8	23	8	24	8	23	9	24	8	23	8	22
1984	6	21	4	19	5	20	4	20	5	21	5	21	7	22	7	23	7	23	8	23	7	22	7	22
1985	5	20	4	19	5	21	5	20	5	21	6	21	7	23	7	23	8	23	8	23	7	22	7	22
1986	5	20	4	19	6	21	5	20	6	21	6	22	7	23	8	23	8	23	8	24	8	22	7	22
1987	6	20	4	19	6	21	5	20	6	21	6	22	7	23	8	24	8	23	9	24	8	23	7	22
1988	6	21	4	19	5	20	4	20	5	21	5	21	7	22	7	23	7	23	8	23	7	22	7	21
1989	5	20	4	19	5	20	5	20	5	21	6	21	7	23	7	23	7	23	8	23	7	22	7	22
1990	5	20	4	19	6	21	5	20	6	21	6	21	7	23	8	23	8	23	8	24	8	22	7	22
1991	6	20	4	19	6	21	5	20	6	21	6	22	7	23	8	23	8	23	9	24	8	23	7	22
1992	6	21	4	19	5	20	4	20	5	21	5	21	7	22	7	23	7	23	8	23	7	22	7	21
1993	5	20	4	18	5	20	5	20	5	21	6	21	7	23	7	23	7	23	8	23	7	22	7	22
1994	5	20	4	19	6	21	5	20	6	21	6	21	7	23	8	23	8	23	8	23	7	22	7	22
1995	6	20	4	19	6	21	5	20	6	21	6	22	7	23	8	23	8	23	9	24	8	23	7	22
1996	6	21	4	19	5	20	4	20	5	21	5	21	7	22	7	23	7	23	8	23	7	22	7	21
1997	5	20	4	18	5	20	5	20	5	21	5	21	7	23	7	23	7	23	8	23	7	22	7	22
1998	5	20	4	19	6	21	5	20	6	21	6	21	7	23	8	23	8	23	8	23	7	22	7	22
1999	6	20	4	19	6	21	5	20	6	21	6	22	7	23	8	23	8	23	9	24	8	23	7	22
2000	6	21	4	19	5	20	4	20	5	21	5	21	7	22	7	23	7	23	8	23	7	22	7	21
2001	5	20																						

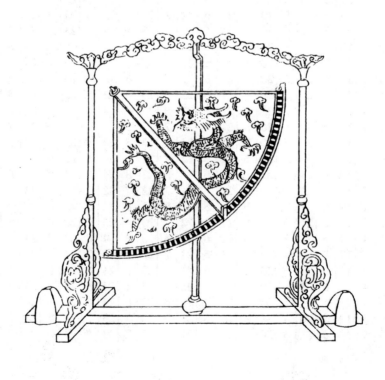

Worksheet 5

Objective

To find the indicator for any day.

Procedure

1. Find the Branch for the Day.
2. Find the date on which the current Monthly Festival commenced.
3. Cross-refer the Branch of the Day with the Monthly Festival in Table XVII to find the Indicator of the Day.

Method

STEP 1. Make a note of the date for which the Indicator is required. [Date].
Enter Date. [**Date**]≫

STEP 2. From Worksheet 1, STEP 23, note the Branch of the Day in question [DB].
Enter Day Branch. [**DB**]≫

STEP 3. Is the [Date] before the 3rd of the month, or later than the 10th? **YES/NO**
If YES, go straight to STEP 6.
If NO, go to STEP 4.

STEP 4. Turn to Table XVI.
Find the line corresponding to the year in question.
Find the nearest date in the table which occurs *before* the [Date] required, and which is a single unit figure.
[Example, Suppose the required date is 23 January 1900. On the 1900 line, there are two January dates: 6th and 20th. The single unit figure is 6.]
Note the number of the Ch'i at the top of the column. (Hint: This number will always be *odd*.)
Enter Ch'i: [**Chi'i**]≫

STEP 5. Turn to Table XVII.
In the second column from the left, find the Ch'i noted in STEP 4. (Ignore the dates in the left-hand column.)
(Go on to STEP 7.)

STEP 6. Turn to Table XVII.
Find, in the left-hand column, the nearest date before the required [Date].

STEP 7. Look along the line and cross-refer to the column headed by the Day Branch ([DB] from STEP 1.)
Note the Letter corresponding to the Indicator for the Day.
Enter the Indicator Letter. [**Indicator**]≫

Interpreting the Twelve Indicators

Once the Indicator has been calculated, the prospects for the day can be ascertained from the following portents.

A: Establish

It is a good day for planning new ventures, but not for putting them into practice. Established businesses will thrive, but neither give nor take credit; deal only in cash or goods. Settle bills. It is good for short journeys on land, but not by boat or by air. On the other hand, it is not a good day for digging or other outdoor activities. Greater success will be achieved through indoor occupations, and matters involving cloth, such as sewing, cutting out, and interior refurbishment will be more rewarding.

Do not draw on savings.

B: Discard

This is not a good day for business or organized social activities, but excellent for spring-cleaning, washing, clearing out and general preparation. Good for any activities concerning one's personal hygiene and appearance. Ideal for visiting the hairdresser, orthodontist, health club, or for sporting activities, particularly swimming.

C: Fullness

This is an excellent day for organizing events, especially social events, on a large scale. Also, long journeys, and time-consuming matters such as moving house may be carried out over the next three days. Wedding receptions, galas, fairs and fêtes are all bound to be successful on this day. The ancient rites seem to have anticipated three-day events, for the next two days are regarded as equally propitious for such large-scale gatherings. It may be best to leave chores unattended if there are more urgent matters needing attention.

It is not regarded as a good day for agriculture or gardening.

D: Even

This is the second day of the three-day festival, and large-scale functions can continue auspiciously.

Those who wisely chose the 'Fullness' day to begin moving house may use this day for interior decoration. Matters concerning the garden, however, are still unfavourably placed.

E: Arrange

The three-day events can be brought to a successful conclusion, while those who were impatient to get back to work can do so. All matters which were left outstanding can now be attacked with renewed vigour.

Keep busy, but mind your own business! If in dispute, keep your views to yourself.

F: Grasp

This is a day best suited for routine work, and for tasks which do not involve moving from one location to another. All matters concerning travel and change of situation are unfavourably aspected. It is not a fortunate day for drawing on resources.

G: Ruin
As the name of the Indicator suggests, this is a day likely to be beset by conflicts. Quiet contemplation, rest or leisure are favoured.

H: Danger
This is a day fraught with problems, and an ever-present danger of accident at work. Another day best suited to leisure – the ancient text goes so far as to suggest that it is advisable to be joyful and drink wine.

I: Completion
This day is favourable for all kinds of activity. Cultivate friendships, avoid gossip and scandal-mongering; speak well of everyone. This is a day when one can start to organize large-scale activities; take out pen, paper and diary, and start planning. It is a good day to begin long journeys; or to begin work which involves digging, such as laying foundations, or turning over the garden.

J: Acceptance
Many of the previous Indicator's activities are also favoured today. Now is probably the best time for calling on one's reserves, or taking out savings, or borrowing in order to start some new project. Commerce and trade are successful.

Organize matters of a joyful nature, but avoid this day for anything to do with health or bereavement. Your genuine Chinese acupuncturist would not be open for consultation on an 'Acceptance' day – the Chinese almanac proscribes acupuncture and moxybustion. From this we can draw the inference that routine visits to the doctor or dentist would not be in order. Also, avoid travel where possible.

K: Open
This is a favourable day for handiwork, and practising crafts – painting, carving or playing muscial instruments. Business dealings, trade and business transactions are favoured.

Travel leads to success. The day favours matters of a happy nature. But avoid the unwholesome or depressing where possible. It would be wrong to arrange funerals or memorials on a day normally associated with joyous events.

L: Shut
This is regarded as a mournful day. It would be a seemly day for funerals, memorial services, erecting monuments, visiting cemeteries and tombs. By extension, it is a good day for saving, hoarding, beginning a diet, or giving up smoking or alcohol.

The Ten-Year Cycle of Fate

In most methods of Chinese astrology, a person's life is divided into ten-year periods, called the 'cycles of fate'. In theory, the *second* of these periods begins at some point during the first ten years of life; thereafter, the fate-cycles follow at intervals of ten years. In other words, if the second fate-cycle began at the age of 3, the third and fourth fate-cycles would begin at the ages of 13 and 23.

The calculations for determining when the fate-cycles begin use the stems of the year of birth, the branch of the month of birth, and the dates of the monthly festivals as the basic criteria. The method for calculating the fate-cycles is described in more detail in Worksheet 6, but for the moment, here are the basic principles.

Chinese astrology teaches that in addition to the universal calendar – the one which is used to date all the events on earth and in the heavens – every individual has a personal calendar, relative to the universal one. It is an astonishing fact that this concept of two kinds of parallel time was expounded some 1,500 years before Einstein's theory of relativity!

These personal 'years' are each ten years long. The twelve branches, which number the (double-)hours of the day are echoed both by the twelve months of the year, and the twelve years of the Great Year. So, by analogy, the ten stems which number the days of the week have a counterpart in the ten-year Cycle of Fate. When this is combined with the twelve branches, it makes an 'epicycle' of 120 years. The Fate Cycle in which a person is born has the same stem-and-branch as the month of birth. Every ten years, as the fate cycle changes, the stem-and-branch moves to the next one. This enables the ages of a person's life to be distributed round the twelve houses of a horoscope chart. Sometimes the stems and branches of the personal Fate Cycle harmonize with those of the calendar year; sometimes they are in conflict. By making a note of the stem and branch of particular years, and comparing these with the stem-and-branch of the personal year at that time, the astrologer is able to note fortunate and unfortunate periods.

Although the Fate Cycle is calculated from the moment of birth, the nine months spent in the womb almost complete the first ten-stem cycle of one's life, so that birth is considered to be a month premature. This is the reason for the second ten-year cycle beginning before ten years of life are complete.

All the Chinese horoscopes which I have examined from the Ming Dynasty onwards mark the respective cycles as years of age on a horoscope chart, either a circular or twelve-sided figure. Thus the chart shows at what age one is likely to encounter serious illness, or travel abroad, for example, by noting the age corresponding to the respective houses – in these cases, the House of Sickness, and the House of Travel.

Worksheet 6 should now be used to calculate the ages which begin each cycle of fate. It could be useful to mark these on a horoscope diagram, such as Horoscope Workchart I. They might conveniently be written outside the framework, leaving the interior of the chart for other calculations.

Worksheet 6

Objective

To calculate a person's Ten-Year Cycles of Fate.

Procedure

STEP 1. Find the stem of the year of birth, and note whether it is yang or yin.

STEP 2. Find the date of the nearest monthly festival
    before the birth-date
        of a male born in a yin year
        of a female born in a yang year

    or
      after the birth-date
        of a male born in a yang year
        of a female born in a yin year

STEP 3. Find the difference between the two dates. This is the 'natal period'.

STEP 4. Divide the natal period by 3. This gives the number of years to the beginning of the *second* Fate Cycle. Note the age at which the second cycle begins.

STEP 5. From the Four Pillars (Worksheet 1) note the stem and branch of the month of birth. This gives the stem and branch of the *first* Fate Cycle.

STEP 6. On the horoscope workchart, note the ages which the person will be at the beginning of each successive ten-year cycle, at those regions which have the same branch as that corresponding to the branch of each ten-year cycle.

Method

STEP 1. Find the following data from Worksheet 1.

    From STEP 6:
        The corrected date of birth [cdb]   [**cdb**]≫

    From STEP 26:
        The stem of the year of birth [YS]   [**YS**]≫
        The stem of the month of birth [MS]   [**MS**]≫
        The branch of the month of birth [MB]   [**MB**]≫

STEP 2. Note whether [YS] is odd or even.
If odd, [A] = 1; if even, [A] = 2.
Enter [A]   [**A**]≫
Note whether the person for whom the horoscope is being cast is male or female.
If male, [B] = 1; if female, [B] = 2
Enter [B]   [**B**]≫

Add [A] + [B] = [C]
Enter [C]   [C] ≫
Note whether [C] is odd or even:

STEP 3.   Turn to Table XVI.
NB. The Monthly Festivals in this table are always those dates which have single unit figures, and are always between 4 and 9.

If [C] is odd,
from Table XVI, find the date of the Monthly Festival immediately before the Corrected Birth Date [cdb].
OR
If [C] is even,
from Table XVI, find the date of the Monthly Festival immediately after the Corrected Birth Date [cdb].

Enter the Monthly Festival Date: **[MFD]**≫

STEP 4.   Note the number of days difference between the corrected birth-date [cdb], and the date of the Monthly Festival [MFD].
This is known as the 'natal period'.
Enter number of days in Natal Period [NP]   **[NP]**≫

STEP 5.   Divide [NP] by 3.
The result gives the number of natal years. (If there is a remainder, take the nearest whole number.)

Enter the number of natal years: [NP] ÷ 3 = [age]   ≫

STEP 6.   The number of natal years gives the age at which the second fate cycle begins.
In the table below, at the top of column B, write the [age].
At the head of the other columns, write the age of the person at ten-yearly intervals.
(*For example, if [age] is 3, write 3 at the head of column B, and 13, 23, 33 . . . at the heads of columns C, D, E . . . etc.*)

STEP 7.   In the table below, in column A, write the stem and branch of the month of birth, [MS] and [MB] from STEP 1 above.

STEP 8.   In the table below, in the second and subsequent columns, increase the value of each stem and branch by 1 for each ten years of age.
(*For example, if the stem and branch entered at Column A is 7-XI, then at columns B, C, D . . . enter 8-XII, 9-I, 10-II . . . etc.*)

STEP 9.   On Horoscope Workchart III outside the perimeter of the diagram, mark the ages which have the same branches as the corresponding regions of the chart.
(*For example, if the branch at the age of 3 is VII, mark 3 on the horoscope chart next to Region VII, and so continue.*)

	A	B	C	D	E	F	G	H
AGE:								
STEM:								
BRANCH:								

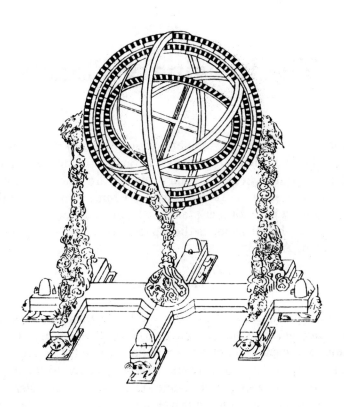

7.

The Imaginary Planets

Although the planets Uranus, Neptune and Pluto were unknown to the founders of Chinese astrology, ancient Chinese horoscopes, at first glance, appear to include a number of planets unknown to us. These 'imaginary' planets are a notable feature of Chinese horoscopes, and their positions are still recorded in Chinese almanacs of the present day.

They are for the most part 'counter-planets' (the meaning of the term will be evident shortly), the most notable of which is the T'ai Sui, or 'Counter-Jupiter', the Reckoner of Years, and God of Astrology.

The T'ai Sui

The planet Jupiter, or 'Year Star' takes about twelve earth-years to complete its circuit of the heavens. Each year the planet appears to have fallen behind by one-twelfth of the heavens, until at the end of twelve years, it has completed its progress through the sky. Thus, it appears to be travelling in the reverse direction to the one in which it is actually going; rather like a slow train being observed from a faster one.

Because the real Jupiter seems to be travelling backwards, another planet, the T'ai Sui, was deemed to travel in the 'correct' direction. Now the twelve positions marked by the T'ai Sui are equal in number to the Monthly Festivals, so that the divisions of the ecliptic into twelve not only reckoned the months of the year, but could also be used as a celestial record of the passage of years. Thus is was that the 'Great Year' of twelve ordinary years was conceived.

(Digressing for a moment, the twelve years are properly marked by the twelve branches, but since about AD 600, it has also become customary in many parts of Asia to call the twelve years by the names of twelve animals – Rat, Ox, Tiger, Rabbit, Dragon, Snake, Horse, Sheep, Monkey, Cock, Dog and Pig – these being easier for lay people to remember.)

In the oldest tables, Jupiter and the T'ai Sui would commence their cycle in the adjacent regions denoted by the branches II and III. The T'ai Sui would then advance by one region in a clockwise direction, and the planet Jupiter in the reverse direction, one region every year.

Today, almanacs mark the position of the T'ai Sui according to the Branch of the year, rather than its reflecting the accurate astronomical position of Jupiter. Theoretically, it ought to be possible to calculate the position of Jupiter from the Branch of the year, given that the T'ai Sui appears in the region which has the same Branch as the year, but the approximation of the Jupiter cycle to twelve years is not sufficiently accurate for the rule to be reliable for more than a generation.

This leads to two positions of Jupiter; the astronomical one, as found by observation (or modern ephemerides) and the notional one, found by inference from the branch of the year.

Other Imaginary Planets

In the same way that Jupiter had its counterpart in an imaginary planet, the T'ai Sui, the other planets too were regarded as having their corresponding 'Evil auras'.

It may be more than a coincidence that Saturn takes approximately twenty-eight years to make a circuit of the heavens, because ancient astronomers, having observed the apparent fall-back of Saturn each year, until after twenty-eight years it came back to its original position, may well have noted its 'stations' by the lunar mansions. Indeed, the twenty-eight lunar mansions may well have been Saturn stations originally.

The position of Saturn could then be calculated in a similar manner to that for finding the position of Jupiter from the year branch, except that the Saturn stations would be derived from a twenty-eight-yearly cycle. Saturn travels so slowly that there would be no difficulty in assigning the start of a twenty-eight-year cycle to a key date, so that a simple calculation would give the right location of Saturn; such a formula would hold good for a century or so.

These rule-of-thumb calculations, however, can only work for the slower-moving outer planets. The inner planets (those between the Earth and the Sun) do not appear to 'fall back', and as a consequence there would be no need to invent imaginary counterparts travelling in the orthodox direction. But to have two planets with their imaginary counterparts, and the other three without them does not satisfy the Chinese philosophy that everything must have its opposite – every yang must have its yin.

The dilemma eventually resolved itself, for, instead of using the Saturn stations, for more than a thousand years, Chinese astrologers have regarded the 'Evil aura' of Saturn as occupying the position of the Moon's descending node, while assigning the corresponding ascending node to the Evil Aura of Mars. This now left the planets Mercury and Venus without their counterparts, or 'evil auras'. Theirs were deemed to be situated directly opposite the positions of their respective planets on the horoscope chart.

Today, the wide availability of accurate ephemerides, and even cheap astrological calculators, means that the positions of the planets can be readily calculated from Western tables, and the data entered onto the horoscopes after conversion to the Chinese system of equatorial degrees.

Converting Western Tables to Chinese Degrees

Three factors are involved in the conversion of Western data to the Chinese system. For most purposes, the conversion table given here will be found to suffice. The figures in this table, however, are rounded to the nearest degree, and some interpolation is required for intermediate figures. Those who wish to work with greater precision will find the appropriate formulae in most manuals of astronomy, the required criteria being the co-ordinates for the position of the star Spica, from which the Chinese scale is reckoned, the angle ε (at present $23\frac{1}{2}°$) for the epoch in question, and the factor 1.0146, to convert Western geometrical degrees to Chinese celestial ones.

Table XVIII: Converting Degrees of the Western Zodiac to Chinese Degrees

To convert the position of a planet given in Western ecliptic degrees to the Chinese equatorial system used in astrology. The first two columns give the Western degrees, firstly in divisions of the great circle of 360 degrees, and secondly as divisions of zodiacal signs. Similarly, the Chinese degrees are given both as divisions of a great circle of 365¼ degrees, and as divisions of the lunar mansions (Hsiu).

The position of a planet or other celestial body on the zodiacal belt can then be found in Chinese degrees, or its lunar mansion, and entered onto the Chinese horoscope chart at the appropriate place.

(The asterisked figures [*1], [*2], etc., represent the lunar mansions.)

Ecliptic degree	Zodiacal degree	Hsiu degree	Equatorial degree	Ecliptic degree	Zodiacal degree	Hsiu degree	Equatorial degree	Ecliptic degree	Zodiacal degree	Hsiu degree	Equatorial degree
0	Aries	11	159	45	15	8	209	85	25	2	246
3	3	14	162	47	17	10	211	87	27	3	247
4	4	*14	164	50	20	13	214	90	Cancer	6	250
5	5	1	165	51	21	*18	215	93	3	*22	253
7	7	3	167	53	23	2	217	95	5	2	255
10	10	6	170	55	25	3	218	97	7	4	257
13	13	*15	173	57	27	5	220	100	10	6	259
15	15	2	175	60	Gemini	8	223	103	13	9	262
17	17	5	178	63	3	*19	226	105	15	12	265
20	20	8	181	65	5	2	228	107	17	14	267
23	23	11	184	67	7	4	230	110	20	16	269
25	25	13	186	70	10	6	232	113	23	19	272
27	27	*16	189	73	13	9	235	115	25	21	274
30	Taurus	3	192	75	15	11	237	117	27	23	276
33	3	7	196	77	17	13	239	120	Leo	25	278
35	5	9	198	80	20	15	241	123	3	28	281
37	7	*17	201	82	22	*20	242	125	5	30	283
40	10	3	204	83	23	1	243	127	7	32	285
43	13	6	207	84	24	*21	244	128	8	*23	286

Ecliptic degree	Zodiacal degree	Hsiu degree	Equatorial degree
130	10	2	288
132	12	*24	290
133	13	1	291
135	15	3	293
137	17	5	295
140	21	7	297
143	23	10	300
145	25	13	303
147	27	*25	305
150	Virgo	3	308
153	3	6	311
154	4	*26	312
155	5	2	314
157	7	5	317
160	10	7	319
163	13	10	322
165	15	12	324
167	17	15	327
170	20	*27	330
173	23	3	333
175	25	6	336
177	27	9	339
180	Libra	12	342
183	3	15	345
185	5	*28	348
187	7	2	350
190	10	5	353
193	13	8	356
195	15	10	358
197	17	13	361
200	20	16	364
201	21	*1	0
203	23	2	2
205	25	4	4

Ecliptic degree	Zodiacal degree	Hsiu degree	Equatorial degree
207	27	7	7
210	Scorpio	10	10
212	2	*2	12
213	3	1	13
215	5	3	15
217	7	6	18
220	10	*3	21
223	13	3	24
225	15	5	26
227	17	7	28
230	20	9	31
233	23	12	34
235	25	13	35
236	26	*4	36
237	27	1	37
240	Sagit.	*5	41
243	3	3	44
245	5	*6	46
247	7	2	48
250	10	4	50
253	13	7	53
255	15	9	55
257	17	11	57
260	20	13	59
263	23	15	62
265	25	*7	64
267	27	1	65
270	Capri.	4	68
273	3	7	71
275	5	10	74
277	7	*8	75
280	10	2	77
283	13	5	80
285	15	7	82

Ecliptic degree	Zodiacal degree	Hsiu degree	Equatorial degree
287	17	9	84
290	20	11	86
293	23	14	89
295	25	16	91
297	27	18	93
300	Aquar.	20	95
303	3	23	98
305	5	25	100
306	6	*9	101
307	7	1	102
310	10	3	104
313	13	7	108
314	14	*10	109
315	15	2	111
317	17	4	113
320	20	6	115
323	23	9	118
325	25	*11	121
327	27	2	123
330	Pisces	5	126
333	3	8	129
334	4	*12	131
335	5	1	132
337	7	4	135
340	10	6	137
343	13	9	140
345	15	11	142
347	17	14	145
350	20	*13	148
353	23	3	151
355	25	5	153
357	27	9	157

Converting Chinese Degrees to Jupiter Stations

The correlation between the Jupiter stations and the lunar mansions varies according to the epoch. The year branch should reveal the position of Jupiter according to the simple formula given earlier, and as the accuracy of this declines over the years, successive historians have had to revise their astronomical tables of correspondences between the T'ai Sui and the position of Jupiter.

In producing tables for modern use, it would be possible either to assign the Jupiter stations to different regions of the heavens, so that the classical formulae for finding the position of Jupiter from the year branch could be retained, or conversely, altering the tables of correspondences between the T'ai Sui and Jupiter, whilst retaining the association of Jupiter with certain lunar mansions, even though these are not consistent in classical writings.

These variations, however, are not so great, and all existing charts, for example, show the first lunar mansion Chio, which represents the Spring Equinox, aligned with Branch IV, Mao, also related to the East and the Spring Equinox. Obviously, it was felt that this correlation, however approximate, should be the one to be retained, and the T'ai Sui tables brought up to date with the present century.

The extraordinary situation now, of course, is that the Jupiter stations, or regions of the horoscope, have been reversed to account for the apparent backward progress of Jupiter, so that in assigning the position of Jupiter to the horoscope, it will be found that Jupiter stations run in the same direction as the T'ai Sui – clockwise. The lunar mansions, however, run in the opposite direction – anticlockwise. A glance at the tables, and Horoscope Workchart II, will make this clear.

Table XIX: Table Showing Correspondence between Lunar Mansion and Jupiter Station

The twelve Jupiter Stations are represented on the horoscope chart by the Twelve Regions. They are fixed places on the horoscope, to which all other factors refer.

BRANCH	MANSIONS from	to	Equatorial degrees		Zodiacal degrees	
I	10-9* →	12-15	118 →	146	323 →	292
II	8-12 →	10-8	87 →	57	291 →	257
III	6-10 →	8-11	56 →	27	256 →	226
IV	3-5 →	6-9	26 →	361	225 →	197
V	28-12 →	3-4	360 →	330	196 →	170
VI	26-17 →	28-11	329 →	300	169 →	143
VII	24-9 →	26-26	299 →	270	142 →	111
VIII	22-16 →	24-8	269 →	239	110 →	77
IX	19-12 →	22-15	238 →	209	76 →	45
X	17-7 →	19-11	208 →	179	44 →	18
XI	15-5 →	17-6	178 →	148	17 →	350
XII	12-16 →	15-4	147 →	119	349 →	324

*i.e. 10th Mansion, 9th degree.

Worksheet 7 – Converting Planetary Positions

Objective

To convert the positions of planetary bodies given in Western tables, into Chinese degrees, with their associated lunar mansions and Jupiter stations.

Procedure

A Western ephemeris, or other means of identifying planetary positions, is required. Once the Western position in zodiacal sign and degrees is known, the conversion is made from Tables XVIII and XIX.

Method

STEP 1. Note the corrected date and time of birth.
From the ephemeris, note the positions of the principal planetary bodies in Column A of the table below.

STEP 2. From Table XVIII, note the corresponding Chinese Lunar Mansion, and degree, and enter into Column B of the table below.

STEP 3. From Table XIX, note the corresponding Jupiter Station for each planet, and enter into Column C of the table below.

PLANET	A		B		C
	Zodiac Sign	Degree	Lunar Mansion	Degree	Jupiter Station
Mercury					
Venus					
Moon					
" asc node					
" desc node					
Mars					
Jupiter					
Saturn					

Table XX: To find the notional position of Jupiter

Column a is the position of the T'ai Sui, which is revealed by the branch of the year.
Column b gives the notional position of Jupiter, according to the ancient Chinese texts.
Column c gives the region occupied by Jupiter for Chinese horoscopes constructed for the present era.

When the T'ai Sui is in region:	Jupiter is in region:	
a	b	c
I	IV	V
II	III	IV
III	II	III
IV	I	II
V	XII	I
VI	XI	XII
VII	X	XI
VIII	IX	X
IX	VIII	IX
X	VII	VIII
XI	VI	VII
XII	V	VI

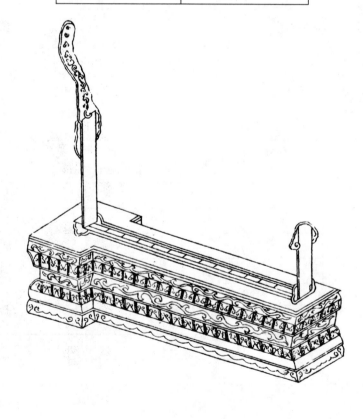

8.

Personality Profiles

Popular astrology tends to concern itself more with personality profiles, rather than prediction, which was astrology's original purpose. The twelve animals of popular Chinese astrology were added to the twelve branches to make the cycle of twelve years easier for the non-Chinese reader to remember. It is apparent that the twelve names were selected by astrologers because those particular animals best represented the qualities of their respective astrological years.

Two examples will suffice to show how the animal names are not only appropriate to the time of day and the season, but are also based on the astrological qualities of the period. The Rat, which is a nocturnal animal, was chosen as the emblem of the midnight hour, and so is associated with the North and Winter. The reader will already have noticed that the first Chinese month of the year does not have the branch I, but III; branch I, which has the symbol of the Rat, now belongs to the eleventh month of the Chinese calendar, approximating to December, and containing the Winter Solstice. The Horse, which symbolizes masculine ambitions and character, is the emblem of noon, when the Sun, or yang force, is at its highest; furthermore, the month of the year which includes the Summer Solstice, VII, by the same reckoning becomes the month of the Horse.

A fuller interpretation of the meanings of the twelve animals in the cycle is beyond the scope of this book, and in any case is exhaustively treated in the wide selection of books available on this subject.* But for the sake of completeness, the principal characteristics of the personality profiles of the twelve animal types is given here.

Rat

Astrological House: Construction
Branch: I
Hour: 11 p.m. – 1 a.m.
Month: 11th (December)

---

*See for example, the present author's *Ming Shu, the Art and Practice of Chinese Astrology* (Pagoda, London, 1987).

Typical years: 1900, 1912, 1924, 1936, 1948, 1960, 1972, 1984
Personality profile: The rat is a nocturnal animal, hence the Rat personality is one who works best at night in the quiet hours. The Rat is studious, persevering, and quick-witted. The Rat is often extremely likeable, characterized by charm and sociability. The Western use of the word 'rat' in a derogatory sense does not apply.

Ox

Astrological House: Construction
Branch: II
Hour: 1 a.m. – 3 a.m.
Month: 12th (January)
Typical years: 1901, 1913, 1925, 1937, 1949, 1961, 1973, 1985
Personality profile: The Ox represents solid dependability, method and routine. Through sheer perseverance, the Ox can succeed where all others fail. Very down-to-earth, cautious and unlikely to take to new ideas.

Tiger

Astrological House: Expansion
Branch: III
Hour: 3 a.m. – 5 a.m.
Month: 1st (February)
Typical years: 1902, 1914, 1926, 1938, 1950, 1962, 1974, 1986
Personality profile: Rash and brash; fiercely competitive, but magnetic. An iron fist in a velvet glove. Proud and defensive, with unpredictable moods. Often enters uniformed services.

Rabbit

Astrological House: Expansion
Branch: IV
Hour: 5 a.m. – 7 a.m.
Month: 2nd (March)
Typical years: 1903, 1915, 1927, 1939, 1951, 1963, 1975, 1987
Personality profile: Benevolent and caring. Often involved in healing, cosmetics, or pharmaceuticals. Avoids confrontation where possible but shows bravery against high odds.

Dragon

Astrological House: Mystery
Branch: V
Hour: 7 a.m. – 9 a.m.
Month: 3rd (April)

Typical years: 1904, 1916, 1928, 1940, 1952, 1964, 1976, 1988
Personality profile: Exotic, wilful, elegant, and with a leaning towards the occult. Tends to make sudden decisions – impulsive, and often short-tempered. Tends to take risks, and often enters the world of entertainment.

Snake

Astrological House: Mystery
Branch: VI
Hour: 9 a.m. – 11 a.m.
Month: 4th (May)
Typical years: 1905, 1917, 1929, 1941, 1953, 1965, 1977, 1989
Personality profile: Quietly methodical, and with a reputation for wisdom. Elegant and epicurean – a connoisseur. Despite this, has a certain naivity, and can be easily scandalized. May turn to fictional writing as a pastime or career.

Horse

Astrological House: Gender
Branch: VII
Hour: 11 a.m. – 1 p.m.
Month: 5th (June)
Typical years: 1906, 1918, 1930, 1942, 1954, 1966, 1978, 1990
Personality profile: The Horse is the symbol of yang or masculine ambitions and possessions. Sociable amongst their own kind, Horse personalities often have difficulties in relating to and understanding the opposite sex. Team sports are preferred to individual attainment.

Sheep

Astrological House: Gender
Branch: VIII
Hour: 1 p.m. – 3 p.m.
Month: 6th (July)
Typical years: 1907, 1919, 1931, 1943, 1955, 1967, 1979, 1991
Personality profile: This is the complementary sign to the Horse, and represents the essence of the yin or feminine. It is a peaceful, retiring and comtemplative sign, and reveals interest in music, poetry and painting. A monastic or contemplative life is often associated with the Sheep.

Monkey

Astrological House: Career
Branch: IX
Hour: 3 p.m. – 5 p.m.

Month: 7th (August)
Typical years: 1908, 1920, 1932, 1944, 1956, 1968, 1980, 1992
Personality profile: While the Horse represented masculine leisure activities, the Monkey represents masculine technological prowess. It shows skills, dexterity and an interest in machines. The character associated with the Monkey shows humour and mischief.

Cock

Astrological House: Career
Branch: X
Hour: 5 p.m. – 7 p.m.
Month: 8th (September)
Typical years: 1909, 1921, 1933, 1945, 1957, 1969, 1981, 1993
Personality profile: This sign reveals aggressive competitiveness. Despite the Cock being a male bird, it represents feminine interests, in particular – fashion, and the garment industry. It is therefore also associated with weaving and embroidery, and to an extent with popular art. The fact that the Cock is associated with the evening hours and the autumn may derive from the fact that the map of the heavens is the reverse of the terrestrial map, so that the dawn and the east on one matches sunset and the west on the other.

Dog

Astrological House: Family
Branch: XI
Hour: 7 p.m. – 9 p.m.
Month: 9th (October)
Typical years: 1910, 1922, 1934, 1946, 1958, 1970, 1982, 1994
Personality profile: The sign of the Dog shows defence, protection and devotion to family. The Dog makes a firm friend, and will stand by loyally when all others have abandoned an apparently hopeless cause. The Dog is usually skilled at matters connected with the fabric or furnishings of a house.

Pig

Astrological House: Family
Branch: XII
Hour: 9 p.m. – 11 p.m.
Month: 10th (November)
Typical years: 1911, 1923, 1935, 1947, 1959, 1971, 1983, 1996
Personality profile: The Pig shows concern for welfare, children and comfort. Pig personalities are drawn towards careers involving young children, such as teaching, nursing and midwifery. Pig personalities are home-makers rather than home-builders.

Compatibility between Signs

Bearing in mind that the compatibility of one 'animal' with another derives ultimately from the harmonies between the branches, it is much more authentic to base an assessment of sign-compatibility on the branches of the birth years. This can be seen immediately from the twelve regions of the horoscope. Those signs which are at right angles in the chart are regarded as forming unfavourable relationships, while those at the 60° or 120° angles are regarded as being harmonious. These angles are identical to the Western astrological teachings regarding the harmonious angles in a planetary chart.

Thus the following groups are regarded as harmonious: Rat-Dragon-Monkey; Ox-Snake-Cock; Tiger-Horse-Dog; Rabbit-Sheep-Pig.

The following groups are regarded as inharmonious: Rat-Rabbit-Horse-Cock; Ox-Dragon-Sheep-Dog; Tiger-Snake-Monkey-Pig.

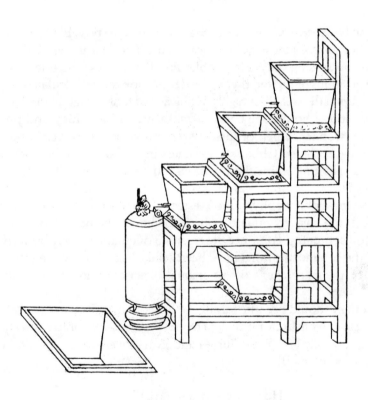

9.

Constructing and Interpreting the Final Horoscope

By now, it will not have escaped the reader that there are two possible courses available for the construction of a Chinese astrological chart. The first is the method used by travelling monks, possessing only a few tables and the Chinese calendar, from which the approximate positions of Jupiter, the Sun and the Moon can be calculated. The second method is to draw upon the wealth of highly sophisticated tables available to the astrologer today, and so produce a horoscope chart of mathematical accuracy and precision.

The reader may wonder which of these two methods is the 'correct' one. No such doubts seem to have bothered Chinese astrologers in the past. The horoscopes which I have examined, spanning more than a thousand years, show Chinese astrologers continually selecting new astronomical discoveries, and adapting them to the traditional methods of astrological philosophy. If the Western student finds it hard to combine the two methods, then the answer, quite simply, is to choose the one with which there is a feeling of greatest sympathy. For, once the essential calculations have been completed, and the keys to the prognostications have been read, every horoscope must bear the eventual stamp of the astrologer's own personal experience and individuality in its interpretation.

Ideally, the student should become familiar with both systems, and for that reason, before attempting to enter astronomical data from Western tables onto a final horoscope chart, all the data compiled from the Tables and Worksheets so far should be entered onto Horoscope Workchart III.

Horoscope Workchart III

Use this workchart to enter the results of all the calculations carried out so far.

The inner ring gives the fixed positions of the twelve regions.

The twelve houses of Fate may now be written into the next circle. These can be calculated from the tables given in the section on the Purple Crepe Myrtle, from Worksheet 2.

The outer circle of segments numbered from 1 to 28 represents the twenty-eight lunar mansions, and the notional or astronomical positions of the Sun, Moon and Jupiter can be written in the appropriate segments next to them. The notional position of the

Horoscope Workchart III

PLANETARY CHART

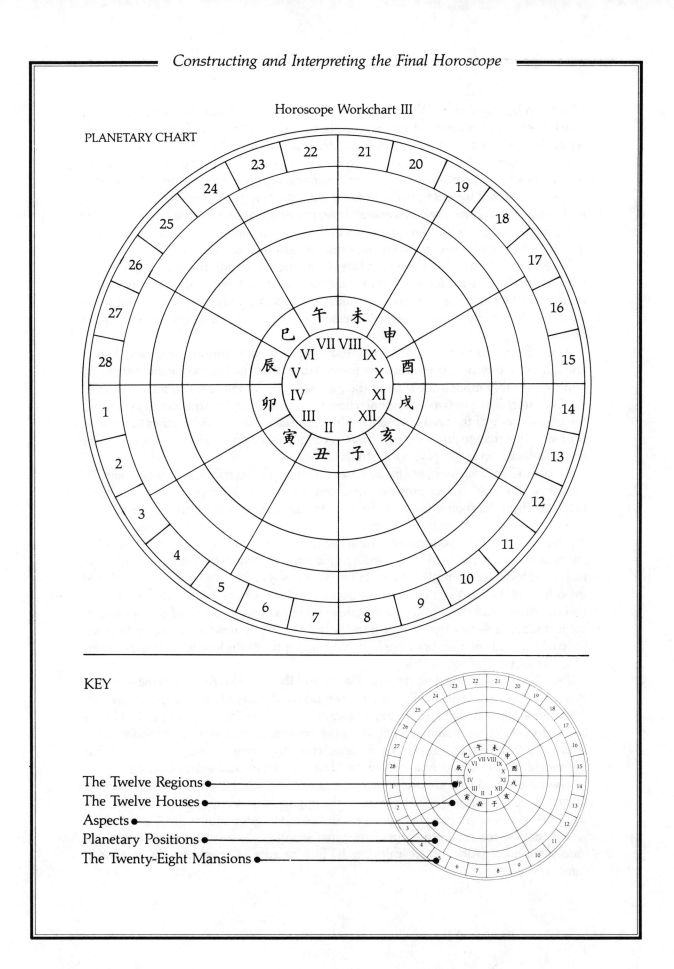

KEY

The Twelve Regions ●
The Twelve Houses ●
Aspects ●
Planetary Positions ●
The Twenty-Eight Mansions ●

Moon can be found from Worksheet 3, and its estimated astronomical position from Worksheet 4. The position of the Sun can be found directly from Table II, column E, while the T'ai Sui and the position of Jupiter is given in Table XX.

In the remaining band, the ages shown by the Fate Cycle can be inserted, so showing the ages at which important events came to bear, this being calculated from Worksheet 6.

Having inserted the data available so far into Horoscope Workchart III, turn back to those sections which give the general meanings of the aspects of the lunar mansions and planets. Note whether Jupiter occurs in the same segment as the Moon; if so, note it in the chart, and write out your own interpretation of the results.

Note the position of the Houses of Fate. Compare them with the notional mansion with which they are associated. Do they appear to have a favourable or unfavourable influence? At what age are the influences likely to be most greatly felt? Again, note down your own interpretation of the aspects formed between the lunar mansions and houses of fate.

Thus, the reader will see that even without recourse to astronomical tables, there is enough astronomical information here for quite a substantial horoscope interpretation, and considerably more if the stars of the Purple Crepe Myrtle are also included. Even so, there are still one or two additional refinements which may be considered to improve the mathematics of the final horoscope, although they add nothing further to the final content, other than to direct the emphasis of certain aspects of the horoscope itself. The first consideration is the place of birth.

Ancient Chinese astrologers made a careful study of the relationships between the lunar mansions and various provinces of China, and by the fifth century it was apparent that an even greater sophistication had entered the calculations, each degree of the heavens being associated with particular localities. But this, of course, was principally for the purpose of forecasting political or natural events. The basis for transferring astrological information onto a personal horoscope is fortunately inherent in the principles laid down in ancient texts. For example, Branch I (Tzu) was always associated with the North and the cold, and Branch VII (Wu) with the South and heat. China lies between the tropics and the Arctic, and the southern hemisphere was unknown to the ancient astrologers. Yet it is reasonable to suppose that if the branches I–VII represent the region between the cold and the heat, then branches VIII–XII must represent the latitudes from the Tropic of Capricorn to the South Pole.

Table XXI correlates each ten degrees of latitude of the inhabited earth with the branches. Perhaps a more mathematically elegant method would accord each degree of latitude with half a horoscope degree, but such a system would be impractical, in view of the large expanses of uninhabited territory at the polar regions, particularly those of the South. Once the relevant region of the horoscope pertaining to the place of birth has been identified, it can be marked on the horoscope chart as the 'natal region'.

The natal region indicates the sphere of action on which the person makes the most impact. It is the response to the subject – the opposite, as it were, of destiny. It is not what life has in store, but what this person has in store for others.

The method for reckoning a person's natal region is so straightforward that it can hardly require a worksheet to calculate it. But for ease of reference, the method is summarized here.

Method of Finding the Natal Region

From an atlas, note the latitude of the person's place of birth. From Table XXI, note the region pertaining to that latitude. Mark the relevant region on the horoscope as being the 'Natal Region'.

The natal region shows the house of destiny on which the subject exerts most influence. For example, if the natal region falls in the House of Brothers and Sisters, it shows the person making a profound impression on his family; if it occurs in a house connected with travel, it does not show that the person would necessarily travel, but that others would be making journeys connected with, or on behalf of, the subject of the horoscope.

Table XXI

Region	Latitude
I	North of the Arctic Circle
II	North of 50°
III	North of 40°
IV	North of 30°
V	North of 20°
VI	North of 10°
VII	Between 10° north and south of the Equator
VIII	South of 10°
IX	South of 20°
X	South of 20°
XI	South of 40°
XII	South of 50°

Establishing the House of Fate

Although a method of establishing the Twelve Houses of Destiny was described in the section on the Purple Crepe Myrtle Genie method of astrology, from the fourteenth century (at the latest) and onward were very much influenced by Western methods of setting up horoscope charts. And although the procedure they used took a different route, the final result was the same. Briefly, it may be said that in Western horoscopes the twelve houses are reckoned from the 'Ascendant' or Rising Sign – the constellation which is on the eastern horizon at the moment of birth.

Chinese horoscopes identify the Midheaven – or position of the heavens which is overhead at the time of birth – as the starting-point of their calculations. The fourteenth-century Chinese horoscopes I have examined all express the Midheaven as degrees of the Chinese lunar mansions, and express this prominently in the centre of the horoscope. In Purple Crepe Myrtle astrology, the 'Midheaven' is indicated by a star called the 'Heaven's Staff' – the staff being, of course, the pointer towards the Midheaven. But then, having established the Midheaven, both the Purple Crepe Myrtle astrology and the horoscopes of the fourteenth century identify as crucial the region which is at Branch IV (Mao). This is the sign associated with the eastern horizon, the first lunar mansion, which now becomes, in consequence, the 'Rising Sign' of the horoscope.

The inference is that whatever method of reckoning is used, the region occupied by the first lunar mansion is where the House of Fate lies.

Hence, the authentic method of finding the House of Fate is to align the lunar mansion occupied by the Sun (so representing the Earth in orbit) with the branch of the birth-time (showing the Earth's rotation). Then the region which holds the House of Fate is the one occupied by the first lunar mansion.

The process could be refined even further by considering the perimeter of Horoscope Workchart II to be divided into Chinese degrees representing the days of the year (which could be found from Column A in Table II), and the horoscopic regions divided into geometric degrees, so that each degree represented four minutes of time.

But the lunar mansion method described here should suffice for virtually all purposes, and is, in any case, a refinement of the Purple Crepe Myrtle method.

As complex as the issue may sound. Worksheet 8 will make the procedure clear.

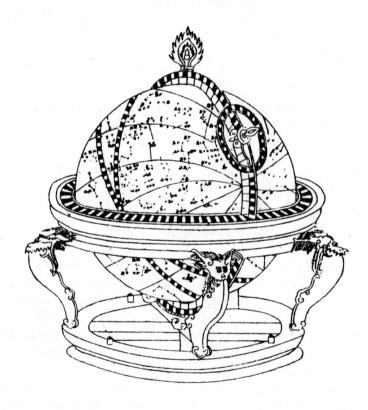

Worksheet 8 – Establishing the House of Fate by the Later Method

Objective

To find the position of the House of Fate, using the methods of later astrologers.

Procedure

1. Find the mansion occupied by the Sun on the day in question.
2. Note the time of birth.
3. Using Workchart IV, align the mansion of the day with the time of birth.
4. Note the *time* which corresponds to the position of the first lunar mansion.
5. The branch corresponding to the position occupied by the first lunar mansion is the number of the region where the House of Fate is situated.

Method

STEP 1.   From Table II, Column E, note the mansion occupied by the Sun on the (corrected) day of birth.
Enter Sun's lunar mansion   **Mansion:≫**

STEP 2.   Turn to Horoscope Workchart IV.
Estimate the position on the dial which is the closest to the corrected time of birth. Mark this position on the edge of the chart.

STEP 3.   The outer band of the chart has 28 blank compartments. Find the one which aligns with the time of birth marked on the Workchart.

STEP 4.   In the compartment corresponding to the time of birth, write the number of the Sun's lunar mansion (from STEP 1).

STEP 5.   Proceeding anticlockwise, write the remaining numbers of the lunar mansions in the outer band of compartments.

STEP 6.   Note the number of the Region (shown by a roman numeral) next to the lunar mansion 1. Between the roman numerals and the outer band of 28 compartments is a band of 12 blank compartments. Write 'Fate' in the blank compartment next to mansion 1.

STEP 7.   Write the names of the other Houses of Destiny in the remaining blank compartments. (These are, in anticlockwise order: Fate, Riches, Kindred, Dwelling, Descendants, Servants, Spouse, Sickness, Removal, Position, Opportunities, Appearance.)

Horoscope Workchart IV

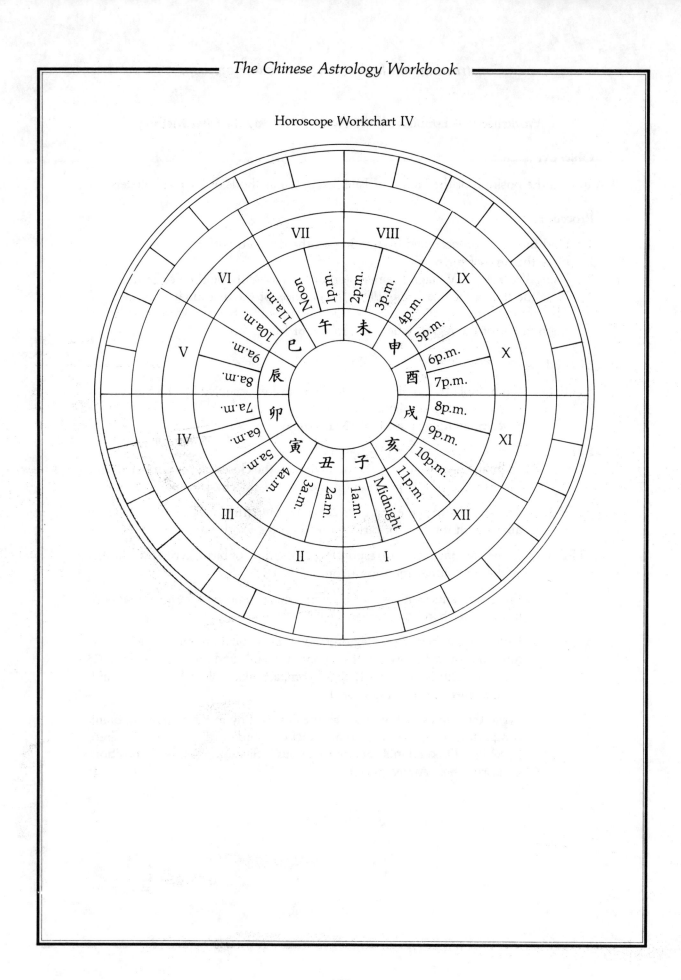

Completing the Chart

We are now ready to turn to the chart itself. Unlike the astrologers of ancient China, the students of today have ready access to accurate and detailed planetary tables; indeed they can even be found in the appendices of several inexpensive compendiums of Western astrology. These tables, or 'ephemerides' will have to be obtained in order to find the astronomical positions of the Moon and planets before they can be converted to the Chinese system for inclusion in the horoscope.

The pattern of the horoscope given here is based on the fourteenth-century work: 'The Treatise on Astrology by Cheng the Sage'. The reader will probably find it helpful to refer to the keyed chart in conjunction with the following notes on its structure. The key letters refer to the following paragraphs.

Key to Horoscope Chart

The Horoscope

(A)   At the top of the chart (see page 127) is a box of eight compartments for the Four Pillars of Fate. It is usual for the name of the person whose horoscope is being cast to be written above this box, together with the given (that is, uncorrected) date, time, and place of birth. The final Chinese date of birth might be written in the centre of the chart. (In the original fourteenth-century horoscopes, this space was used for noting the Midheaven. Present-day readers, however, will probably feel that their Chinese date of birth has greater relevance in this type of horoscope.)

Any amendments, notes, and corrections should always be done on separate sheets of paper (such as the worksheets) so leaving the chart for the end results of any calculations.

(B)   The outer band of the chart contains the names of stellar deities; in this workbook, we have used the eighteen stars of Purple Crepe Myrtle astrology.

(C)   There are two undivided blank bands, an 'outer' and an 'inner'. This 'outer' blank band is for noting favourable or adverse aspects of the Purple Crepe Myrtle stars and planets, and any other information of note.

(D)   The next band is a grid divided into three rows of 120 degrees. Its purpose is to identify the locations of the planets on the horoscope as nearly as possible. The first degree of the band is that corresponding to the first degree of the first lunar mansion, so it will not be possible to enter the planetary positions until the positions of the lunar mansions have been established.

(E)   The positions of the twenty-eight lunar mansions are inserted in the 'inner' blank band, using the twelve divisions of the grid as a guide. Of course, once this has been done, the planetary positions can then be inserted into the grid itself.

(F)   The twelve blank compartments are used to denote the Houses of Destiny, which can only be written in once the region of the Fate has been established.

(G)   In the remaining blank area, the ages of the ten-year Fate Cycle are inserted at the appropriate place. The Natal Region is also marked in this band.

(H)   The central band of Chinese characters shows the twelve branches, representing the twelve 'regions' of the horoscope. They are always in this position, with Region I at the bottom.

Worksheet 9, which revises all the techniques needed to construct the horoscope, should now be used in order to practise completing the chart.

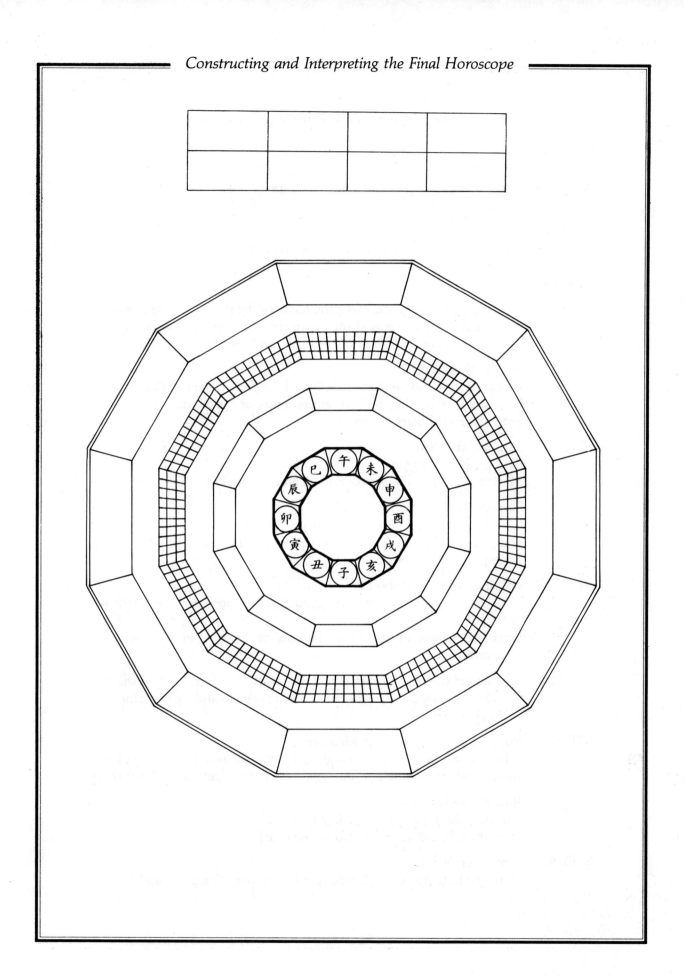

Worksheet 9 – Completing the Chart

Objective

To complete a chart for final presentation and interpretation.

Procedure

Assimilate all the data calculated so far onto the final chart.

Method

STEP 1.   Take a copy of the chart. Write the name of the person whose horoscope is being cast (the *querent*) at the top of the chart, together with the given (i.e. uncorrected) date and time of birth, and the place of birth.

STEP 2.   Turn to Worksheet 1.
Calculate the Chinese date of birth and the Four Pillars of Fate.
Enter the Chinese date of birth at the centre of the chart.
Enter the Four Pillars in Box A.

STEP 3.   Turn to Table XXI.
Find the Natal Region.
Mark a pointer at the appropriate degree in Band G of the chart.

STEP 4.   Turn to Worksheet 8.
Calculate the positions of the twenty-eight lunar mansions.
Transfer the positions of the lunar mansions to Band E of the chart, at the corresponding degree points.

STEP 5.   Continue with Worksheet 8.
Mark the House of Fate by writing *Fate* in the appropriate compartment of Band F.
Enter the names of the other Houses of Destiny in the remaining compartments.

STEP 6.   Take an ephemeris, or other planetary tables, and turn to Worksheet 7.
Calculate the planetary positions in Chinese degrees and complete the table in Worksheet 7.

STEP 7.   Note the position of Lunar Mansion 1.
Using the position of Lunar Mansion 1, enter the positions of the planets on the grid as accurately as possible, within the limitations of the chart.

STEP 8.   Turn to Worksheet 2.
Calculate the positions of the Eighteen Stars.
Enter these in the outer Band B of the chart.

STEP 9.   Turn to Table VII.
Mark the positions of Fortunate and Unfortunate Stars in Band C.

STEP 10. Turn to Worksheet 6.
          Calculate the Ten-Year Fate Cycle, and enter the relevant ages at their respective places, also in Band C.

STEP 11. Turn to Worksheet 3.
          Calculate the Notional Mansion for the day, and write this at the foot of the chart.

STEP 12. Turn to Worksheet 5.
          Calculate the Indicator for the day, and write this at the foot of the chart.

The technical matters of erecting the horoscope are now complete, and the horoscope ready for the astrologer's interpretation.

Interpreting the Horoscope

Now that the horoscope has been constructed, it has to be interpreted, in order that the revelations of the celestial messengers be comprehensible. The person who asks for a horoscope in order to find out what Fate has in store is more likely to be bewildered than impressed by a wealth of technical terms and data. Those who want to know if they will become wealthy, those who hope to make a good marriage, and those who wish to achieve fame are unlikely to glean much from being told that the Purple Crepe Myrtle is in its Temple in the House of Removal.

The worksheets in this book have been prepared to assist the student through the technical processes of calculating a horoscope. The interpretation of the aspects and portents, however, is very much more an intuitive process, and although guidelines to the development of a predictive faculty have been given in every section, the final completion of the horoscope would appear to be an appropriate place to revise the key pointers in its interpretation.

There are, in fact, two sets of indications, due to the fact that the Chinese astrological chart is of complex origin. Certain aspects will be shown by the Purple Crepe Myrtle, calculated according to the itinerant astrologer's methods, and the other is the sophisticated planetary chart, based on highly precise astronomical tables. The advised course to take is to make the first assessment of the portents based on astronomical data, and then to turn to the Purple Crepe Myrtle, the Notional Lunar Mansion, and the Indicator for the day for the answer to any outstanding matters which may remain. The following course is suggested.

First of all, note the Natal Region, which shows the area which the subject will have most influence on. This might be the subject's family, or career, or business, although the full implications of the Natal Region may only be apparent later when the final picture begins to emerge.

Next, deal with the Purple Crepe Myrtle indications, noting where successes and dangers are likely to be found. The general tone of the Indicator for the day, and the Notional Lunar Mansion, should be jotted down.

The key to the whole process of interpretation, however, lies in the Twelve Houses of Destiny. Study these in conjunction with the lunar mansions in which they are found. Decide what implications each lunar mansion may have for each of the twelve houses. If for example, Mansion 28, the Carriage, is found in the House of Removal, this would seem to be a sure indication that the subject would be destined to lead a travelling life.

Now note which planets are present in each House of Destiny. The more planets are present in a house, the greater will be the impact of the events or circumstances to which that house refers.

If there is more than one planet present in a region, note (from the interaction of the Five Elements) whether the conjunction is favourable or not. Consider what the effect of the planets is in the mansions where they are found, and whether the combination of planet and mansion is favourable or not. Then, as a definite picture begins to take form, the age at which the event is likely to take place can be judged from the ten-yearly cycles of fate.

Appendix:
Worked Examples of Worksheets and Workcharts

Worksheet 1
(See page 20ff.)

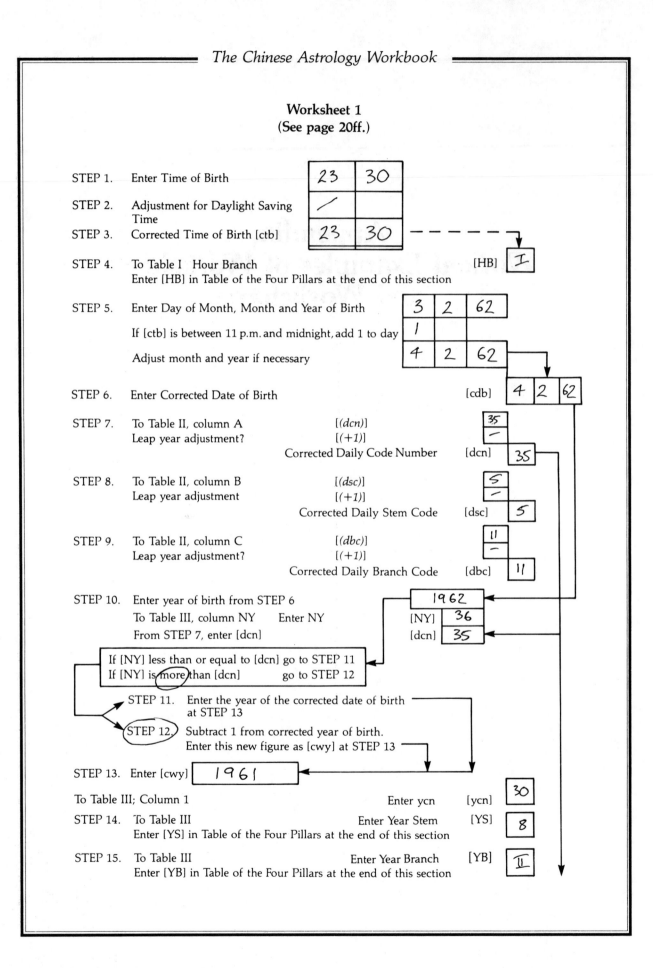

STEP 1. Enter Time of Birth

23	30

STEP 2. Adjustment for Daylight Saving Time

STEP 3. Corrected Time of Birth [ctb]

23	30

STEP 4. To Table I Hour Branch
Enter [HB] in Table of the Four Pillars at the end of this section   [HB]   I

STEP 5. Enter Day of Month, Month and Year of Birth

3	2	62

If [ctb] is between 11 p.m. and midnight, add 1 to day   1

Adjust month and year if necessary

4	2	62

STEP 6. Enter Corrected Date of Birth   [cdb] | 4 | 2 | 62 |

STEP 7. To Table II, column A   [(dcn)]   35
Leap year adjustment?   [(+1)]   —
Corrected Daily Code Number   [dcn]   35

STEP 8. To Table II, column B   [(dsc)]   5
Leap year adjustment   [(+1)]   —
Corrected Daily Stem Code   [dsc]   5

STEP 9. To Table II, column C   [(dbc)]   11
Leap year adjustment?   [(+1)]   —
Corrected Daily Branch Code   [dbc]   11

STEP 10. Enter year of birth from STEP 6 | 1962 |
To Table III, column NY   Enter NY   [NY]   36
From STEP 7, enter [dcn]   [dcn] 35

If [NY] less than or equal to [dcn] go to STEP 11
If [NY] is more than [dcn]   go to STEP 12

STEP 11. Enter the year of the corrected date of birth at STEP 13

STEP 12. Subtract 1 from corrected year of birth.
Enter this new figure as [cwy] at STEP 13

STEP 13. Enter [cwy] | 1961 |

To Table III; Column 1   Enter ycn   [ycn]   30

STEP 14. To Table III   Enter Year Stem   [YS]   8
Enter [YS] in Table of the Four Pillars at the end of this section

STEP 15. To Table III   Enter Year Branch   [YB]   II
Enter [YB] in Table of the Four Pillars at the end of this section

STEP 16. To Table IV Enter common year name [CY]

Metal	Ox

STEP 17. To Table III: (central block of figures)
Enter Monthly Code Number [mcn] | 6 |

STEP 18. To Table III, head of column
Enter Chinese Lunar Month [LM] | 12 |

STEP 19. To Table III, foot of column
Enter Monthly Branch [MB] | II |

Enter [MB] in Table of Four Pillars at the end of this section

STEP 20. [dcn] − [mcn] | 35 | − | 6 | [   ] | 29 |

if [dcn] − [mcn] 31 or more, subtract 31   [(−31)]

Add 1 [+1] | 1 |

Chinese Day of Lunar Month [CD] | 30 |

| 30 | | 12 | | Metal - Ox |

STEP 21. The Chinese Date is [CD] day of [LM] month in [CY] year

STEP 22. Enter [dsc] [dsc] | 5 |
Enter [ycn of Western (uncorrected) year] [ycn] | 35 |
[dsc] + [ycn] = [   ] | 40 |
Divide by 10 = [   ] | 40 |
Remainder is Day Stem [DS] | 0 | 10 |

Enter [DS] in Table of the Four Pillars at the end of this section

STEP 23. Enter [dbc] [dbc] | 11 |
Enter [ycn of Western (uncorrected) year] [ycn] | 35 |
[dbc] + [ycn] = [   ] | 46 |
Divide by 12 = [   ] | 36 |
Remainder is Day Branch [DB] | 3 | 10 |
Enter [DB] in Table of the Four Pillars at the end of this section

STEP 24. To Table V. From [HB]/[DS] Read Hour Stem | I | 10 | [HS] | 9 |
Enter [HS] in Table of the Four Pillars at the end of this section

STEP 25. To Table VI. From [MB]/[YS] Read Month Stem | II | 8 | [MS] | 8 |
Enter [MS] in Table of the Four Pillars at the end of this section

STEP 26. Enter the Stem and Branch of Hour, Day, Month, Year.

Table of the Four Pillars

[HS]	[DS]	[MS]	[YS]
9	10	8	8
[HB]	[DB]	[MB]	[YB]
I	X	II	II

✓

Worksheet 2
(See page 52ff.)

Objectives

1. To establish the positions of the Fixed Stars.
2. To establish the positions of the Fate and Associated Houses.

Procedure

1. From Worksheet 1 note the Hour Branch, Year Branch, Day of the Chinese Month, and Chinese Lunar Month.
2. Note the positions of the twelve principal stars, and enter these on the horoscope chart, inner ring.
3. Note the positions of the auxiliary stars, and note these on the horoscope chart, second ring.
4. Note the auspices, Temple, Radiance and Pleasure of the stars.
   Find the position of the Fate Palace.
5. Note the position of the Twelve Houses on the outer ring of the horoscope chart.

Method

STEP 1. From Worksheet 1, STEP 26, note the following data:
Hour Branch [HB]≫ I
Year Branch [YB]≫ II

STEP 2. From Worksheet 1, STEP 20, note the following data.
Chinese Day of Month   [CD]≫ 30 th
The number of the Chinese Lunar Month   [LM]≫ 12 th

STEP 3. Use the Year Branch [YB] to find the Region occupied by the Purple Star [*a] as follows:

[YB] → I (II) III IV V VI VII VIII IX X XI XII
VIII (IX) X XI XII I II III IV V VI VII → Purple Star Region

Enter the Purple Star [*a] into its appropriate region in the Inner Ring on Horoscope Workchart II.

STEP 4. Assign the eleven remaining principal stars [*b] to [*l] round the Inner Ring of Horoscope Workchart II.

STEP 5. Use the number of the Chinese Lunar Month of birth [LM] to find the region occupied by Heaven's Staff [*m] as follows:

[LM] → 1 2 3 4 5 6 7 8 9 10 11 (12)
I XII XI X IX VIII VII VI V IV III (II) → Heaven's Staff

Enter the Heaven's Staff [*m] into its appropriate regions in the Second Ring of Horoscope Workchart I.

STEP 6. Assign the auxiliary stars Heaven's Curiosity [*n], Hair and Fur [*o] and Heaven's Axe [*p] to the Second Ring of Horoscope Workchart I, in the three regions following Heaven's Staff [*m] in anticlockwise order.

STEP 7. Use the number of the Chinese Lunar Month of birth [LM] to find the region occupied by Heaven's Punishment [*q] as follows:

[LM] → 1 2 3 4 5 6 7 8 9 10 11 ⑫
       X XI XII I II III IV V VI VII VIII ⟨IX⟩ → Heaven's Punishment

Enter the Heaven's Punishment [*q] into its appropriate region in the Second Ring of Horoscope Workchart I.

STEP 8. Use the number of the Chinese Lunar Month of birth [LM] to find the region occupied by Heaven's Elegance [*r] as follows:

[LM] → 1 2 3 4 5 6 7 8 9 10 11 ⑫
       XII I II III IV V VI VII VIII IX X ⟨XI⟩ → Heaven's Elegance

Enter the Heaven's Elegance [*r] into its appropriate region in the Second Ring of Horoscope Workchart I.

STEP 9. Use the Branch of the Year of Birth [YB] to find the region occupied by Heaven's Lamenting [*s] as follows:

[YB] → I ⟨II⟩ III IV V VI VII VIII IX X XI XII
       II ⟨I⟩ XII XI X IX VIII VII VI V IV III → Heaven's Lamenting

STEP 10. From Table VII, note the Fortunate and Unfortunate stars, and mark these into the Horoscope Workchart I in the appropriate places on the Third Ring.

STEP 11. From Table IX, note the Temple, Radiance and Pleasure of the stars, and enter these into the appropriate regions of the Third Ring in Horoscope Workchart I.

STEP 12. Using the birth hour branch [HB] and the position of the Heaven's Staff [*m], find the position of the Fate Palace from Table X. Enter the Fate Palace into its appropriate region of the Outer (fourth) ring of Horoscope Workchart I.

STEP 13. From Table XI, note the positions of the eleven remaining Houses of Fate, and enter these on to Horoscope Workchart I.

STEP 14. Using the Day of the Chinese Lunar Month [CD], and the region occupied by Heaven's Staff [*m], find, from Table XII, the region of the Body Palace. Mark this on Horoscope Workchart I.

STEP 15. Now analyse the horoscope according to the principles outlined in the section 'Interpreting the Fate' (page 44).

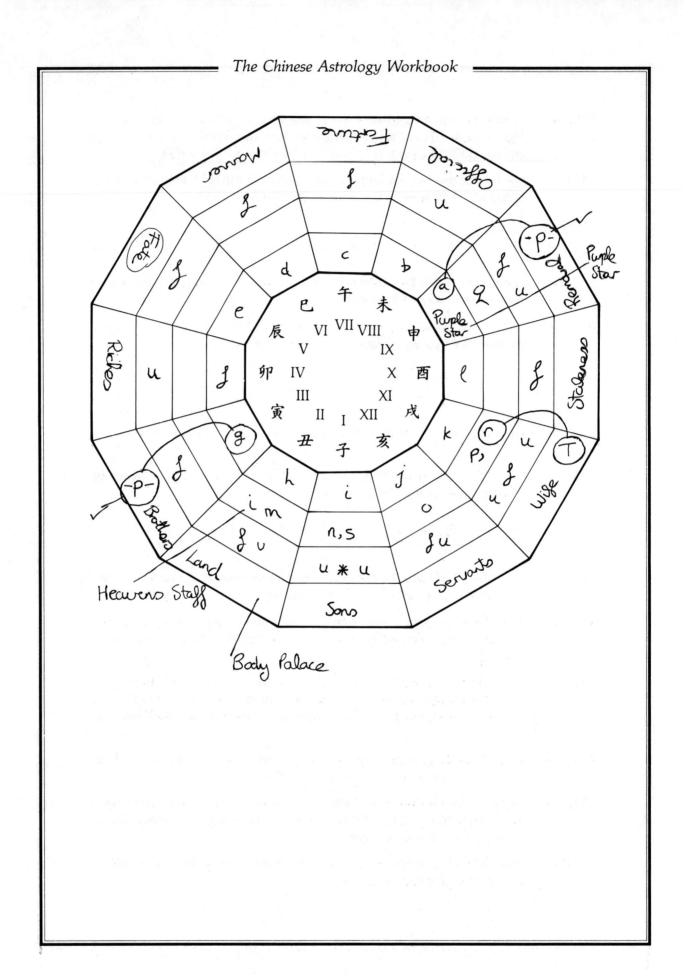

Worksheet 3 – Calculating the Notional Mansion for any day
(See page 59)

Objective

To calculate the Notional Mansion for any day.

Procedure

Add the codes for the year and date, with a leap-year adjustment if necessary.
If the total is greater than 28, subtract 28; the result is the number of the Notional Mansion.

Method

STEP 1. Note the date for which the Notional Mansion is required. 4 -2 -62
From Table II (page 26-8) Column D, note the Code Number for the day.
[a]≫ 7

STEP 2. From Table XIII on page 60, note the Code Number for the year. [b]≫ 25

STEP 3. If the date in question is 29 February or later in a leap year, add 1, otherwise
add 0. [c]≫ 0

STEP 4. Add (a) + (b) + (c). [d]≫ 32

STEP 5. If (d) is greater than 28, subtract 28 and note the remainder. Otherwise enter
(d). [e]≫ 4

STEP 6. The figure at (e) is the number of the Notional Mansion. ≠The Room

Worksheet 4 – Estimating the Moon's Position
(See page 62ff.)

Objective

To estimate the mansion occupied by the Moon on any day.

Procedure

1. Find the mansion occupied by the Sun on the day in question.
2. Calculate the Chinese date according to Worksheet 1.
3. Find the nearest date which would be the 15th day of the Chinese month.
4. Enter the position of the Sun on the 15th day on the Chart of the Lunar Mansions.
5. Count the number of days to the day in question.
6. Count the same number of degrees from the solar position.
7. Take the point on the chart directly opposite the solar position to give the lunar position of the day in question.

Method

STEP 1.   Enter the date for which the Moon's lunar mansion is required. **date≫** 4 :2 :62

STEP 2.   From Table II (page 26), Column A, note the Daily Code Number (amended if necessary to account for dates occurring in a leap year on or after 29 February) **A [dcn] of date≫** 35

STEP 3.   From Table III (page 28), Central Block, find the line of figures corresponding to the year of the required date.
   Find the figure which is the nearest one below the Daily Code Number. (NOTE: Ignore the right-hand figure 1 in the split columns for the eleventh and twelfth months.)
   Enter nearest monthly code number: **B≫** 6

STEP 4.   Add 15 to the nearest monthly code number.
   Enter [B] + 15 = **C≫** 21

STEP 5.   Return to Table II. Find the date which corresponds to the figure C. This is the date of the Full Moon closest, or next closest, to the required date.
   Enter date of Full Moon: **Full Moon≫** 21 : 1

STEP 6.   Note the number of days difference between the required date and the date of the Full Moon, and whether the Full Moon is before or after the date in question.
   Enter number of days: **Difference ≫** 14
   Enter 'before' or 'after' **Before/after ≫** after

STEP 7.   From Table II, column E, find the number of the Solar Mansion on the day of the Full Moon.
   Enter Solar Mansion: **Solar Mansion ≫** 8

STEP 8.   From Table II, column E, look upwards along column E and count the number of days on which the Sun was in the same solar mansion prior to the date of the Full Moon, to give the Solar Mansion Degrees.
Enter number of days: **Solar Mansion Degrees** ≫ **23**

Now Turn to Horoscope Workchart II

STEP 9.   On Horoscope Workchart II, find the segment corresponding to the Solar Mansion, calculated above in STEP 7.
Find and mark the point on the scale equal to the Solar Mansion Degrees in STEP 8.

STEP 10.   Place a ruler or straight edge on the chart, and mark the point on the scale directly opposite the Solar Mansion Degrees. This gives the position of the Full Moon.
Find and mark the position of the Full Moon.

STEP 11.   On the central, blank band of Horoscope Workchart II, note the segment corresponding to the position of the Full Moon.

STEP 12.   Refer to STEP 6 and note the Difference, and before/after:
Difference ≫ **23 Before/after** ≫ *after*

On the central, blank, band of the chart, count out as many divisions as the Difference.
Count anticlockwise for 'before' and clockwise for 'after'.
The corresponding mansion on the outer band is the mansion occupied by the Moon on the day in question.

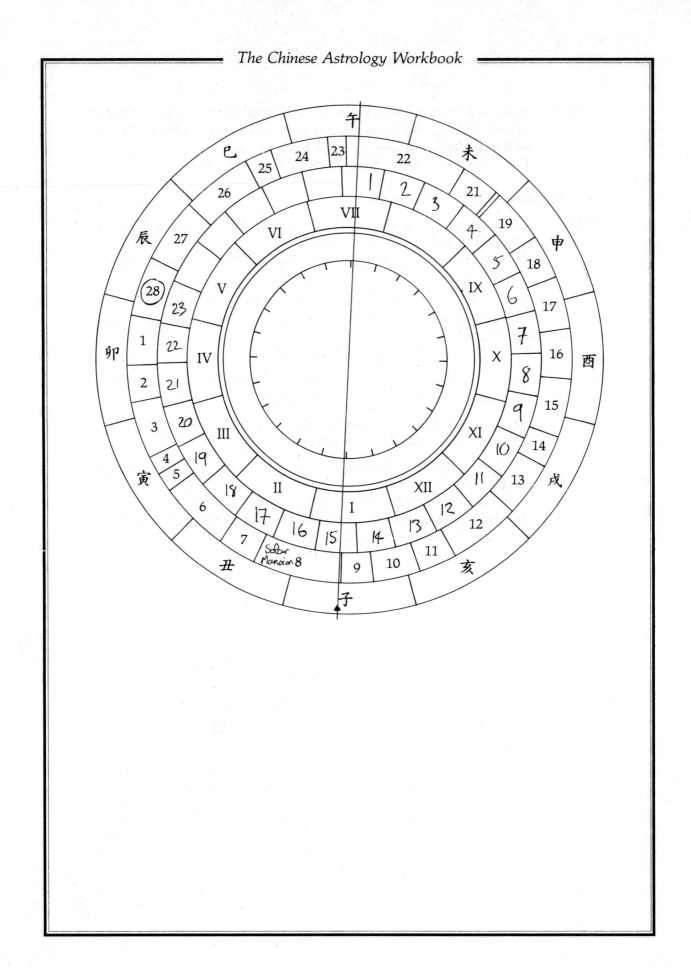

Worksheet 5
(See page 101)

Objective

To find the indicator for any day.

Procedure

1. Find the Branch for the Day.
2. Find the date on which the current Monthly Festival commenced.
3. Cross-refer the Branch of the Day with the Monthly Festival in Table XVII to find the Indicator of the Day.

Method

STEP 1.   Make a note of the date for which the Indicator is required. [Date].
Enter Date.   [**Date**]≫   4-2-62

STEP 2.   From Worksheet 1, STEP 23, note the Branch of the Day in question [DB].
Enter Day Branch. [**DB**]≫ ⚊

STEP 3.   Is the [Date] before the 3rd of the month, or later than the 10th?   **YES/NO**
If YES, go straight to STEP 6.
If NO, go to STEP 4.

STEP 4.   Turn to Table XVI.
Find the line corresponding to the year in question.
Find the nearest date in the table which occurs *before* the [Date] required, and which is a single unit figure.
[Example, Suppose the required date is 23 January 1900. On the 1900 line, there are two January dates: 6th and 20th. The single unit figure is 6.]
4th Feb. Note the number of the Ch'i at the top of the column. (Hint: This number will always be *odd*.)
Enter Ch'i: [**Ch'i**]≫   /

STEP 5.   Turn to Table XVII.
In the second column from the left, find the Ch'i noted in STEP 4. (Ignore the dates in the left-hand column.)   /
(Go on to STEP 7.)

STEP 6.   Turn to Table XVII.
Find, in the left-hand column, the nearest date before the required [Date].

STEP 7.   Look along the line and cross-refer to the column headed by the Day Branch ([DB] from STEP 1.)
Note the Letter corresponding to the Indicator for the Day. *H*
Enter the Indicator Letter. [**Indicator**]≫ *Danger* .

Worksheet 6
(See page 105ff)

Objective

To calculate a person's Ten-Year Cycles of Fate.

Procedure

STEP 1. Find the stem of the year of birth, and note whether it is yang or yin.

STEP 2. Find the date of the nearest monthly festival
　　　　before the birth-date
　　　　　　of a male born in a yin year
　　　　　　of a female born in a yang year

　　　　or
　　　　after the birth-date
　　　　　　of a male born in a yang year
　　　　　　of a female born in a yin year

STEP 3. Find the difference between the two dates. This is the 'natal period'.

STEP 4. Divide the natal period by 3. This gives the number of years to the beginning of the *second* Fate Cycle. Note the age at which the second cycle begins.

STEP 5. From the Four Pillars (Worksheet 1) note the stem and branch of the month of birth. This gives the stem and branch of the *first* Fate Cycle.

STEP 6. On the horoscope workchart, note the ages which the person will be at the beginning of each successive ten-year cycle, at those regions which have the same branch as that corresponding to the branch of each ten-year cycle.

Method

STEP 1. Find the following data from Worksheet 1.

　　　　From STEP 6:
　　　　　　The corrected date of birth [cdb]　　[cdb]≫ 4 - 2 - 62

　　　　From STEP 26:
　　　　　　The stem of the year of birth [YS]　　[YS]≫ 8
　　　　　　The stem of the month of birth [MS]　　[MS]≫ 8
　　　　　　The branch of the month of birth [MB]　　[MB]≫ 丑

STEP 2. Note whether [YS] is odd or even.
　　　　If odd, [A] = 1; if even, [A] = 2.
　　　　Enter [A]　[A]≫ 2
　　　　Note whether the person for whom the horoscope is being cast is male or female.
　　　　If male, [B] = 1; if female, [B] = 2
　　　　Enter [B]　[B]≫ 1

Add [A] + [B] = [C]
Enter [C]   [C]≫ 3
Note whether [C] is odd or even: odd

STEP 3.   Turn to Table XVI.
NB. The Monthly Festivals in this table are always those dates which have single unit figures, and are always between 4 and 9.

If [C] is odd,
from Table XVI, find the date of the Monthly Festival immediately before the Corrected Birth Date [cdb].
OR
If [C] is even,
from Table XVI, find the date of the Monthly Festival immediately after the Corrected Birth Date [cdb].

Enter the Monthly Festival Date: **[MFD]**≫ 4 - 2 - 62

STEP 4.   Note the number of days difference between the corrected birth-date [cdb], and the date of the Monthly Festival [MFD].
This is known as the 'natal period'.
Enter number of days in Natal Period [NP]   **[NP]**≫ O

STEP 5.   Divide [NP] by 3.
The result gives the number of natal years. (If there is a remainder, take the nearest whole number.)

Enter the number of natal years: [NP] ÷ 3 = [age] ≫ O

STEP 6.   The number of natal years gives the age at which the second fate cycle begins.
In the table below, at the top of column B, write the [age].
At the head of the other columns, write the age of the person at ten-yearly intervals.   birth
(*For example, if [age] is 3, write 3 at the head of column B, and 13, 23, 33 . . . at the heads of columns C, D, E . . . etc.*)

STEP 7.   In the table below, in column A, write the stem and branch of the month of birth, [MS] and [MB] from STEP 1 above.

STEP 8.   In the table below, in the second and subsequent columns, increase the value of each stem and branch by 1 for each ten years of age.
(*For example, if the stem and branch entered at Column A is 7-XI, then at columns B, C, D . . . enter 8-XII, 9-I, 10-II . . . etc.*)

STEP 9.   On Horoscope Workchart III outside the perimeter of the diagram, mark the ages which have the same branches as the corresponding regions of the chart.
(*For example, if the branch at the age of 3 is VII, mark 3 on the horoscope chart next to Region VII, and so continue.*)

	A	B	C	D	E	F	G	H
AGE:	/	0	10	20	30	40	50	60
STEM:	10	1	2	3	4	5	6	7
BRANCH:	X̅	X̅I̅	X̅I̅I̅	I̲	I̲I̲	I̲I̲I̲	I̲V̲	V̲

Worksheet 7 – Converting Planetary Positions
(See page 113ff)

Objective

To convert the positions of planetary bodies given in Western tables, into Chinese degrees, with their associated lunar mansions and Jupiter stations.

Procedure

A Western ephemeris, or other means of identifying planetary positions, is required. Once the Western position in zodiacal sign and degrees is known, the conversion is made from Tables XVIII and XIX.

Method

STEP 1.   Note the corrected date and time of birth.
From the ephemeris, note the positions of the principal planetary bodies in Column A of the table below.

STEP 2.   From Table XVIII, note the corresponding Chinese Lunar Mansion, and degree, and enter into Column B of the table below.

STEP 3.   From Table XIX, note the corresponding Jupiter Station for each planet, and enter into Column C of the table below.

PLANET	A		B		C
	Zodiac Sign	Degree	Lunar Mansion	Degree	Jupiter Station
Mercury					
Venus					
Moon					
″ asc node					
″ desc node					
Mars					
Jupiter					
Saturn					

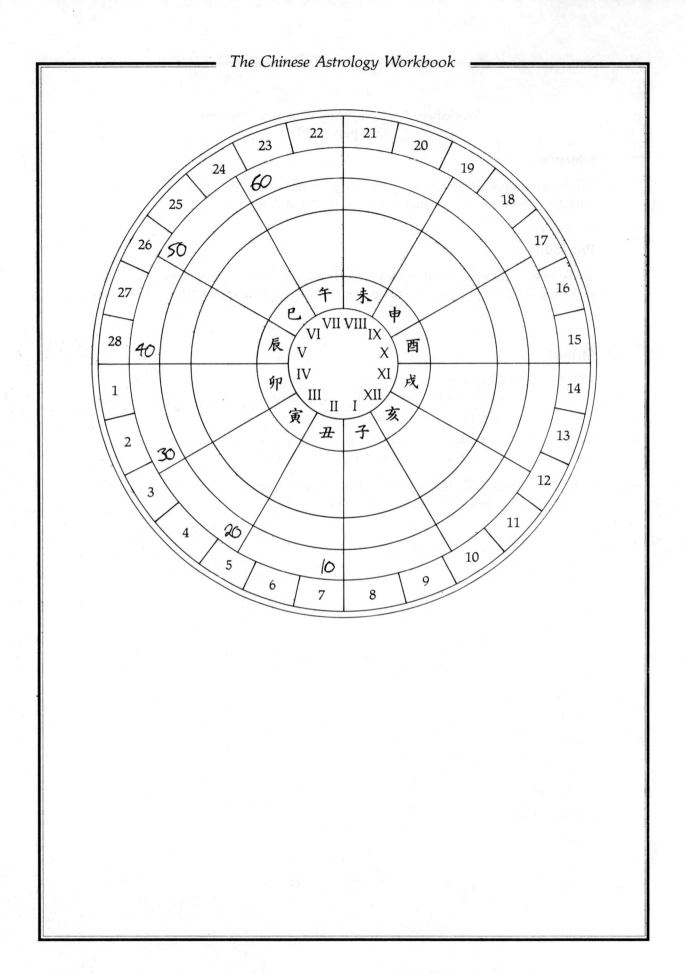

Worksheet 8 – Establishing the House of Fate by the Later Method
(see page 125)

Objective

To find the position of the House of Fate, using the methods of later astrologers.

Procedure

1. Find the mansion occupied by the Sun on the day in question.
2. Note the time of birth.
3. Using Workchart IV, align the mansion of the day with the time of birth.
4. Note the *time* which corresponds to the position of the first lunar mansion.
5. The branch corresponding to the position occupied by the first lunar mansion is the number of the region where the House of Fate is situated.

Method

STEP 1.   From Table II, Column E, note the mansion occupied by the Sun on the (corrected) day of birth.
Enter Sun's lunar mansion   **Mansion:≫**

STEP 2.   Turn to Horoscope Workchart IV.
Estimate the position on the dial which is the closest to the corrected time of birth. Mark this position on the edge of the chart.

STEP 3.   The outer band of the chart has 28 blank compartments. Find the one which aligns with the time of birth marked on the Workchart.

STEP 4.   In the compartment corresponding to the time of birth, write the number of the Sun's lunar mansion (from STEP 1).

STEP 5.   Proceeding anticlockwise, write the remaining numbers of the lunar mansions in the outer band of compartments.

STEP 6.   Note the number of the Region (shown by a roman numeral) next to the lunar mansion 1. Between the roman numerals and the outer band of 28 compartments is a band of 12 blank compartments. Write 'Fate' in the blank compartment next to mansion 1.

STEP 7.   Write the names of the other Houses of Destiny in the remaining blank compartments. (These are, in anticlockwise order: Fate, Riches, Kindred, Dwelling, Descendants, Servants, Spouse, Sickness, Removal, Position, Opportunities, Appearance.)

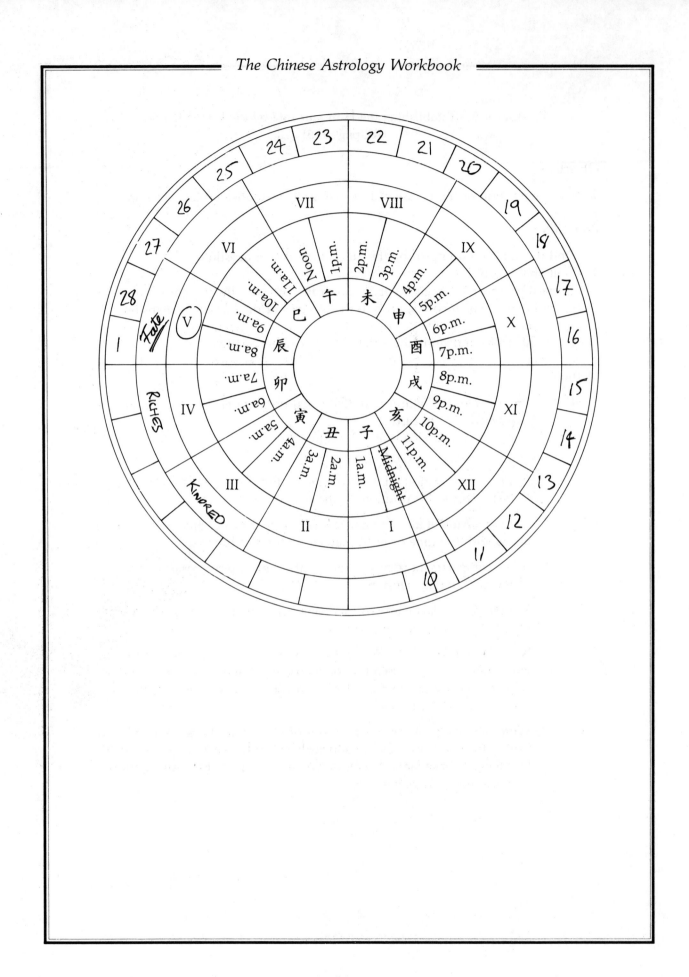

Worksheet 9 – Completing the Chart
(See page 130ff)

Objective

To complete a chart for final presentation and interpretation.

Procedure

Assimilate all the data calculated so far onto the final chart.

Method

STEP 1. Take a copy of the chart. Write the name of the person whose horoscope is being cast (the *querent*) at the top of the chart, together with the given (i.e. uncorrected) date and time of birth, and the place of birth.

STEP 2. Turn to Worksheet 1.
Calculate the Chinese date of birth and the Four Pillars of Fate.
Enter the Chinese date of birth at the centre of the chart.
Enter the Four Pillars in Box A.

STEP 3. Turn to Table XXI.
Find the Natal Region.
Mark a pointer at the appropriate degree in Band G of the chart.

STEP 4. Turn to Worksheet 8.
Calculate the positions of the twenty-eight lunar mansions.
Transfer the positions of the lunar mansions to Band E of the chart, at the corresponding degree points.

STEP 5. Continue with Worksheet 8.
Mark the House of Fate by writing *Fate* in the appropriate compartment of Band F.
Enter the names of the other Houses of Destiny in the remaining compartments.

STEP 6. Take an ephemeris, or other planetary tables, and turn to Worksheet 7.
Calculate the planetary positions in Chinese degrees and complete the table in Worksheet 7.

STEP 7. Note the position of Lunar Mansion 1.
Using the position of Lunar Mansion 1, enter the positions of the planets on the grid as accurately as possible, within the limitations of the chart.

STEP 8. Turn to Worksheet 2.
Calculate the positions of the Eighteen Stars.
Enter these in the outer Band B of the chart.

STEP 9. Turn to Table VII.
Mark the positions of Fortunate and Unfortunate Stars in Band C.

STEP 10.   Turn to Worksheet 6.
Calculate the Ten-Year Fate Cycle, and enter the relevant ages at their respective places, also in Band C.

STEP 11.   Turn to Worksheet 3.
Calculate the Notional Mansion for the day, and write this at the foot of the chart.

STEP 12.   Turn to Worksheet 5.
Calculate the Indicator for the day, and write this at the foot of the chart.

The technical matters of erecting the horoscope are now complete, and the horoscope ready for the astrologer's interpretation.

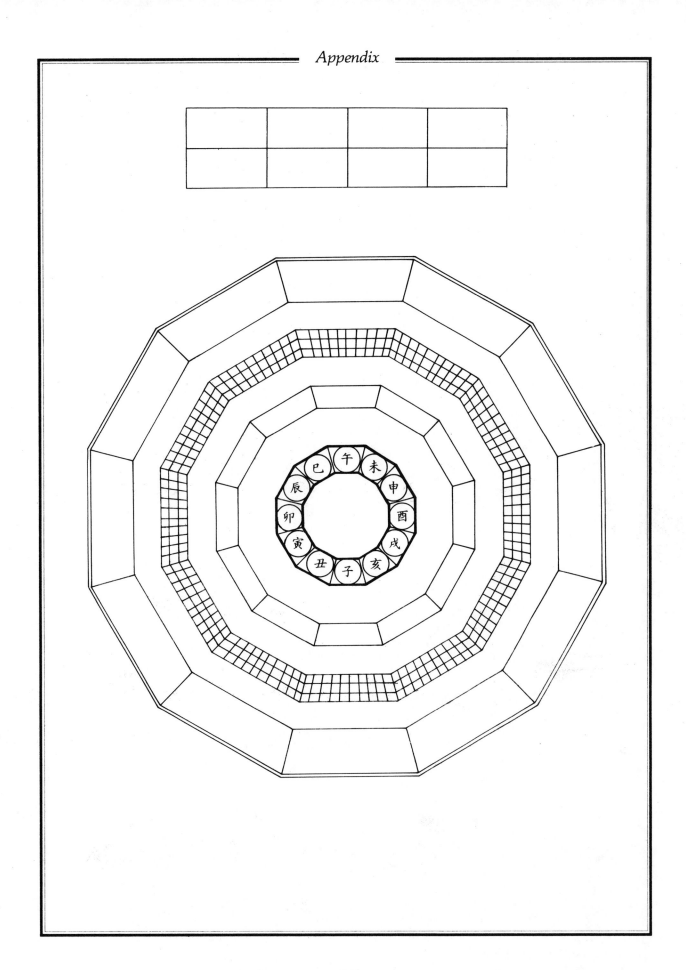

Glossary

Animals — (Twelve). Animal names have been used as a popular alternative to the Twelve **Branches** for more than a thousand years. They were originally used to identify the twelve years of the Great Year, but are often used additionally for the Chinese double-hours, and occasionally for the months of the year as well. They are: Rat, Ox, Tiger, Rabbit, Dragon, Snake, Horse, Sheep, Monkey, Cock, Dog, Pig. See pages 18 and 115.

Branch — One of twelve signs used by the Chinese for numbering divisions of time, in particular the double-hours, months, and years of the Jupiter cycle. In this book, the convention is adopted of using the roman numerals I to XII for the branches, so distinguishing them from the ten **Stems**. See page 15.

Ch'i — Literally, 'breath'. One of twenty-four divisions of the solar year, also known as 'fortnights' or 'solar terms'. Two Ch'i make a **Festival**.

Chieh — See **Festival**.

Counter-Jupiter — An imaginary planet considered to orbit the Sun in the opposite direction to Jupiter in order to account for the fact that Jupiter appears to fall back from its appointed place by one-twelfth of the heavens each year. See **Jupiter Cycle**.

Ecliptic — The path taken by the Sun (and more widely, the planets) through the sky. So called because it is only when the Moon crosses this path that an eclipse can occur. Also see **Equator**.

Element — One of five fundamental forces – Wood, Fire, Earth, Metal and Water, identified with the planets Jupiter, Mars, Saturn, Venus and Mercury respectively. See page 78.

Ephemeris — A set of tables for calculating the positions of planets and other celestial bodies for a particular time and day.

Equator — (Celestial Equator). The great circle imagined to mark the circumference of the heavens, at right angles to a line joining the celestial pole to the earth's pole. In Chinese astronomy, it is divided unequally into twenty-eight by the lunar **Mansions**. See also **Ecliptic**.

Equinox — One of two days in the year when day and night are of equal length. They usually occur on 21 March and 21 September. Compare **Solstice**.

Festival — (Chieh). One of twelve exact divisions of the solar year, consisting of two **Ch'i**. They

155

are the nearest equivalent to the signs of the Western zodiac, each Festival taking the latter half of one Western zodiacal sign, and the beginning half of the next.

Great Bear Astrology — See **Tzu Wei.**

Great Year — See **Jupiter Cycle.**

House — (of Destiny). One of twelve areas of a person's life, associated with various regions of the sky according to the date and time of one's birth. The twelve houses are: Fate; Riches and Wealth; Brothers and Kindred; Land and Dwelling; Sons and Daughters; Servants and Slaves; Wife and Concubines; Sickness and Distress; Removal and Change; Official and Reward; Good Fortune and Virtue; Manner and Bearing. See page 39ff.

Jupiter Cycle — As the planet Jupiter takes twelve years to orbit the heavens, its positions in the sky match those of the Sun throughout the year. This led to the concept of a **Great Year** formed of twelve earthly years. These twelve years were originally numbered by the **Branches** but later the names of twelve 'zodiacal' animals were added.

Mansion — Or 'lunar mansion'. In this book, the term 'mansion' is used for one of the departments of the sky, divided from the Pole Star to the Celestial Equators into twenty-eight unequal segments. See page 54ff.

Notional — Theoretical, as distinct from actual. For example, the 'notional' lunar mansion is the theoretical position of the Moon, derived from traditional calculations, rather than the one actually occupied by the Moon.

Palace — The term 'Palace' is used frequently in Chinese astrological textbooks to mean a department of the heavens or the horoscope. It might apply to divisions of the sky (the Purple Palace being the area round the North Pole Star) or some division of the horoscope, such as the Houses of Destiny. In this book, the word Palace has been translated variously according to context, to reduce confusion.

Pillar — One of the four divisions of the date and time of birth – the hour, the day, the month and the year – expressed as a stem and branch formula. See page 8.

Purple Crepe Myrtle — See **Tzu Wei.**

Querent — The subject of the horoscope, i.e. the person whose horoscope is being cast.

Region — One of twelve fixed divisions of the horoscope, numbered, clockwise, from the bottom centre, and identified by the twelve **Branches.** See page 35.

Root Direction — This curious term is a direct translation from the Chinese. It refers to the **House of Destiny** dealing with the **Querent's** particular question.

Solar Terms — See **Ch'i.**

Solstice — One of two days of the year when the daylight is at its maximum (Summer Solstice) or minimum (Winter Solstice). Compare **Equinox.**

Station — (Jupiter Station). The part of the sky to which Jupiter returns every twelve years. As the twelve years are reckoned by the twelve **Branches** the terms are sometimes interchangeable. See **Jupiter Cycle.**

Stem — One of ten signs used by the Chinese for numbering divisions of time, originally used for days, and now combined with the **Branches** to make a cycle of sixty combinations. In this book, the convention adopted is to use the ordinary numerals 1 to 10 for the stems, so distinguishing them from the branches, for which roman numerals are used. See page 15.

T'ai Sui — (Pronounced like the English words *tie sway*.) Literally, the Great Year. See **Jupiter Cycle**.

Ten-Year Cycle (of Fate) — A ten-year period of a larger cycle of 120 years. The ten-yearly fate cycles point to significant stages in a person's life. See page 103.

Tzu Wei — (Pronounced *tsoo way* or in Cantonese *chee way*.) Literally, the Purple Crepe Myrtle. The name of a spirit whose residence is the seven major stars of the Great Bear. Tzu Wei astrology is based on calculating the influences of the particular fixed stars and meteors, rather than the motions of the planets. See pages 33ff.

Zodiac — In Western astrology, a band of constellations, most of which are named after animals (hence *zoo-diac*), which traces the paths taken by the Sun and planets through the sky. The term should be avoided when speaking of Chinese astrology, as it might be taken to mean either the names of the **Twelve Animals** or the twenty-eight **Mansions** along the celestial **Equator**.

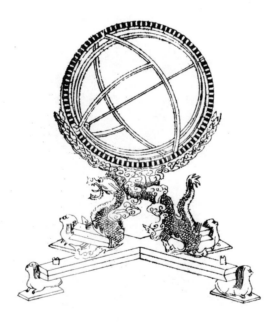

Index

Of further interest . . .

CHINESE ASTROLOGY
(An Aquarian Astrology Handbook)

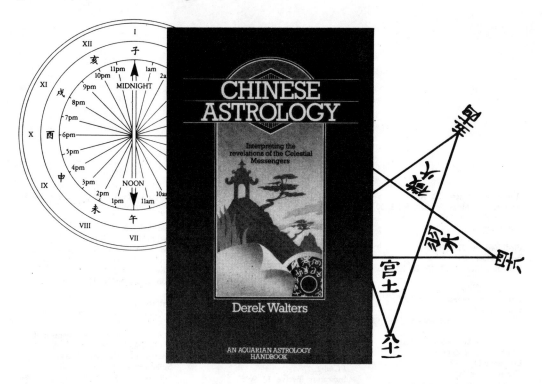

Interpreting the revelations of the Celestial Messengers

Derek Walters

The Chinese have practised astrology for many thousands of years. They had compiled a systematic method of observing and interpreting the heavens long before contact had been made with the western world.

CHINESE ASTROLOGY is the first comprehensive study of this fascinating subject to be made available in a western language. The author traces the history of Chinese Astrology from its earliest records to the present and explains the principles on which the art is founded. The subject is brought to life by the inclusion of a number of actual Chinese horoscopes from different periods. Among the many astrological texts which are quoted is the complete two-thousand year old treatise written by the Grand Astrologer, Ssu Ma Ch'ien.

Derek Walters is Europe's foremost authority on Chinese Astrology, respected not only for his thorough academic knowledge of the subject, but also as an actual practitioner of Chinese Divination. He writes frequently for a leading astrological magazine, and has appeared on British radio and television.